THE FUNDAMENTALS OF ENGLISH GRAMMAR

DR. PRABHAT CHOURASIA

Made with ❤ on the Notion Press Platform
www.notionpress.com

I dedicate this book to my wife and my daughter whose time I stole to translate my long lived craving to write this book. I also dediate this book to all my students, teaching whom I got the inspiration to write it.

Contents

Foreword   vii

Preface   ix

Acknowledgements   xi

Prologue   xiii

1. The Sentence   1

2. Nouns   24

3. Adjective   72

4. Articles   107

5. Pronouns   115

6. Verb   127

7. Adverbs   141

8. Prepositions   153

9. Conjunction   162

10. Interjections   173

11. Tense   181

12. Direct And Indirect Speech   193

13. Active And Passive Voice   208

14. Common Errors (subject-verb Agreement)   217

Foreword

Grammar is the backbone of any language. A language without grammar is like a body without soul. All the four basic skills i.e., listening, speaking, reading and writing depend upon one's knowledge of English grammar. Error free verbal communication is the need of the hour in this era of 21st century globalisation, English is the second language in most of the countries across the globe. It gives you an access into the fast-growing areas to place yourself as a professional. I found this book very useful not only for students but for everyone in the society.

Preface

Fundamentals of English Grammar and Composition caters the need of Indian students who are in Secondary and Senior-Secondary classes. This book has separate sections dealing with grammar, vocabulary, comprehension and composition. So, the teachers do not need to look for additional books to teach reading and writing skills or to enhance their students' vocabulary.

This book is based on the Sumption that our students do not need to study grammar as a subject in its own right. They need to study grammar so that they can express themselves correctly, unambiguously, coherently, and persuasively. Its aim is not to master English grammar, but to learn English as a language and grammar is to be used as an essential aid to that. So, I decided to give them grammar in action, that is, define and explain essential grammatical concepts with the help of lucid illustrations and follow them up with a variety of exercises to strengthen conceptual grasp. This is the approach we have followed throughout the series. Some unique features of the grammar section are:

- Concepts have mostly been presented graphically and have been highlighted so that they stand out on the printed page.
- Tips to write correctly and alerts to avoid common errors have also been highlighted. Both teachers and students will find these tips extremely useful.
- There are review sections to evaluate learning outcomes.
- Exercises are significantly large in number and are well graded. There is also a great deal of a variety in them. These exercises will enable the teachers to build up an activity-based approach towards teaching grammar and make it and enjoyable class experience.
- Exercises have been designed to generate positivity among the students and to include ethical values in them without their being conscious of it.

I had a two-fold am in the section dealing with composition: Students should be able to use their imagination and organise their thoughts. Illustrative material provided by me, as well as the exercise listed for the students should help in the realization of their aim.

Dr. Prabaht Chourasia

11.01.2023

Acknowledgements

This book is based on my experience with my students and the people I met in the way of my life. Grammar is not all about mugging up its rules but to know how to use them. I would like to thank my wife and daughter whose precious time I stole to make this book a reality. I would also like to thank the people of my organization who have always motivated me to write this book.

Prologue

Grammar is the soul of any language. its absence or wrong use may damage a language like anything. There are various chapters which deal in details the fundamental rules of English grammar which are not there in other books in the present era.

CHAPTER ONE

The Sentence

A. The Sentence

Look at the following groups of words:

1. played evening last we a match hockey
2. did match team the win your

These groups do not make any sense. Let us rewrite them as:

1. We played a hockey match last evening.
2. Did your team win the match?

Now they make complete sense.

- A group of words that makes complete sense is called a sentence.

We must not forget four things about a sentence:

- A sentence makes complete sense.
- It begins with a capital letter.
- The words in a sentence must be in their proper order.
- A sentence ends with a full stop, a mark of interrogation, or a mark of exclamation.

A.   The Phrase

Some groups of words make sense, but not complete sense.
For example,

1.   a funny story
2.   last evening
3.   at the bus stop
4.   of no use

- a group of words that makes sense but not complete sense is called a phrase.

Note that just any group of words cannot be described as a phrase. A phrase must have some sense:
played a hockey --- not a phrase a hockey match---- phrase.
We can turn a phrase into a sentence by adding some words to
it:

1.   My mother told me a funny story last evening.
2.   I shall wait for you at the bus stop.
3.   This book is of no use to me.

- A sentence always has a verb in it. In fact, the verb is at the heart of a sentence.

Exercise 1. Put a tick (√) against the groups of words which are sentences and a cross (✗) against those which are not:

1.   The whole school beautifully decorated.
2.   Essays is the of the this better to the.
3.   This is the better of the two essays.
4.   The whole furniture in the various rooms of the school across the river.
5.   Go.

6. Being tired of waiting for the train.
7. We were tired of waiting for the train.
8. The colonies across the railway line.
9. Have across houses line the very colonies the big.
10. The colonies across the railway line have very big houses.

Exercise 2. Make sentences using the following phrases:

1. Full of beautiful pictures
2. Ups and downs of the
3. In a hurry
4. In good health
5. Covered with mud
6. Two hours late
7. Advantages and disadvantages
8. Liked by many people
9. In a courteous manner
10. Without any fear

C. Parts of a Sentence

A sentence is made up of two parts: subject and predicate.

- Subject ---- that part of a sentence which names what the sentence is about.
- Predicate ---- that part of the sentence which says something about the subject.

For example,

All the players contributed to the victory of the team. In this sentence *All the players* is subject and *contributed to the victory of the team* is predicate.

- The verb is an essential part of the predicate.

- In an imperative sentence, the subject is always 'you', but it is implied and not stated.

For example,

1. Sit down. (You sit down.)
2. Open your book at page 28. (You open your book at page 28.)

Exercise 3 Draw one line under the subject and two lines under the predicate:

1. Several herbal plants grown in our kitchen garden have great medicinal properties.
2. Tulsi is one of them.
3. Eat a couple of tulsi leaves every day to remain healthy.
4. Drinking large quantities of water removes toxic substances from our body.
5. We must not drink water from a pond or a lake.
6. Pond water is not fit to drink.
7. On the topmost shelf of my cupboard lies a big red book.
8. This book gives very useful health tips.

D. Kinds of Sentences

Sentences are of four kinds:

1. Assertive or declarative sentences
2. Interrogative (questions)
3. Imperative (command, instruction, advice, request)
4. Exclamatory (exclamation)

E. Positive or Declarative Sentences (Statements)

- An assertive or declarative sentence says or states something.

Assertive sentences are of two kinds:

1. Affirmative or Positive
2. Negative

For example,

1. The fox looked at the piece of cheese. (affirmative)
2. The fox did not like it. (negative)

We put a full stop at the end of an assertive sentence.

F. Interrogative Sentences (Questions)

- An interrogative sentence asks a question.

Interrogative sentences are also of two kinds:

1. Yes/No question
2. Wh-questions

For example,

1. Do you like stories?
2. What kind of stories do you like?

Sentence 1 above is a yes or no question. It means that this kind of questions can be answered in yes or no. Such a question begins with an auxiliary verb, In sentence 1 above, so is an auxiliary verb.

For the teacher:

Auxiliary verbs are verbs used to form the tenses and voices of other verbs. Be, do, have and modals (can, may, will, shall etc.) are auxiliary verbs. They are also called helping verbs.

Sentence 2 begins with a question word (What). Since most of the question words what, when, where, who, whose, whom, why begin with Wh, such questions are often referred toas wh-questions. These questions cannot be answered in yes or no. some statements have to be made to answer them.

In an interrogative sentence, the auxiliary verb is placed before the subject.

For example,

1. They have gone away. (statement)
2. Have they gone away? (question)
3. He has read the novel. (statement)
4. Has he read the novel? (question)

Two things to remember about an interrogative sentence:

- In an interrogative sentence, we put the auxiliary verb before the subject.
- We put a mark of interrogation (?) at the end of an integrative sentence.

G. Wh-questions

Wh-questions begins with:

1. Interrogative pronouns: who, whose, whom, what, which.
2. Interrogative adjectives: what colour, which child, whose turn.
3. Interrogative adverbs: when, where, why, how, how long, how far, how often, how soon.

Interrogative pronouns:

- Who, whose, whom apply only to persons:

1. Who has taken my pen? Surabhi has taken it.
2. Whose is this book? It is so Surabhi's.
3. Whom do you want to meet? I want to be Gerald.

- Who is used as a subject; whom is used as an object:

1. Who invited you?
2. Whom are you inviting?

Hobby bird these days. In informal conversation, it is usual to use who instead of whom:

1. Whom do you want to talk to?
2. Who do you want to talk to?

Both the sentences given above are now accepted as correct. The first one is more formal. In written English, we prefer this form. The second one is informal. In spoken English, we often use this form.

- What can be used for persons as well as things:

1. What is in your pocket? My handkerchief. (a thing)
2. What is he? He's a teacher. (a person)

Look at these two questions and their answers:

1. Who is he? He is a friend.
2. What is he? He is a businessman.

When we use what with a person, it means that we want to know his trade or profession.

- Which applies both to persons and things. We use which when we have to select some person or thing from a given group.

1. Who is the captain? (general inquiry)
2. Which of you is the captain? (pointing to a group)

Interrogative Pronouns

- Who, whose, whom .... only persons
- What which .... persons as well as things
- Who .... used as subject
- Whom .... used as object

Exercise 4 Fill in the blanks with suitable *question words*:

1. .... has been appointed the head girl?
2. .... of these clubs would you like to join?
3. .... serials do you like to watch?
4. .... did you manage to keep everybody happy?
5. Your school is so far away............ don't you shift to the hostel?
6. .... do you want to meet? (formal)
7. .... are these picture tubes imported from?

H. Imperative Sentences (Commands)

- An imperative sentence expresses a command or order, an instruction, a request, or an advice.

For example,

1. Keep off the grass. (command)
2. Put this notice on the notice board. (instruction)
3. Pause me the sugar, please. (request)
4. Do your homework regularly. (advice)

For the teacher:
Whether an imperative sentence is an order request, et cetera depends often upon the speaker's tone. Command does not necessarily suggest an order. It includes all the four ideas —order, instruction, request advice.

I. Exclamatory Sentences (Exclamations)

* An exclamatory sentence expresses some strong feeling, surprise, excitement, etc.

For example,

1. How beautiful double fly is!
2. What a nuisance it is!
3. Oh, what a lovely sight!
4. Amazing shot!

Note that in order to make an exclamatory sentence forceful, we use a slightly different word order. In sentence 1, the normal word order should have been:
It is (what) a nuisance.

* We put a mark of exclamation (!) at the end of an exclamatory sentence.

Exercise 5. The words in the following groups can we rearrange to form either a statement or a question. Write out both the statement at the question:
Example,
Is of very noodles child fond this
This child is very fond of noodles. (statement)
Is this child very fond of noodles? (question)

1. insects the is of one wonderful ant the most
2. sorry news the get she to illness was of my
3. tired, poor, hungry the thirsty was woodman and
4. help done work she anybody's entire the has without
5. zoo are there strange in many the animals
6. heal caused by difficult wounds to are harsh words

7. satisfaction John able your your will entire be to problem solve to

8. should tablets she doctor by take all the the suggested

Exercise 6. Rearrange the words in the following groups to make each group an interrogative sentence.
Example,
When you will return these books?
When will you return these books?

1. how long you have been living here
2. why you are angry with Sanjay
3. where you have hidden all the toys
4. how I can accept such a proposal
5. when you will go to bed
6. how many brothers and sisters you are
7. why you are disturbing me
8. how much money I should give you

Exercise 7. Rearrange the words in the following groups to make each one a command, instruction, request, or advice. In some of the sentences, you will have to insert a comma.
Example,
flowers this not black garden do from
Do not pluck flowers from this garden.

1. money do borrow lend not on
2. anybody rudely never with talk
3. at carefully boys look the blackboard
4. a near Lucy classroom don't noise the make
5. sir me answer let try to this question
6. running lean of do bus out not a window of
7. warm day a water take three tablets times this with
8. on carefully instructions the follow the written bottle

Exercise 8. Rearrange the words in the following groups to make them proper exclamatory sentences:
Example,
how is lovely rose the
How lovely the rose is!

1. made speech she boring a what
2. how well-behaved those and children disciplined were
3. interesting what an is story this
4. wearing a beautiful what was she dress
5. manager how did one tactfully assistant interrogate
6. was the pleasant how the weather hills on
7. what she a argument gave strong

Exercise 9. Rewrite the following passage using capital letters and putting in a full stop, a mark of interrogation or a mark of exclamation (but no comma) where necessary:

One day when Suheena was coming home from school, she saw magician there was a big crowd around him he filled a glass with ink and covered it with a piece of red cloth then he chanted some magic words and pulled away the clothes what a surprise the ink had turned into rose petals Suheena immediately thought of her sick grandfather would not this trick make him smile would not it reduce his pain Suheena learned the magic words from the magician and rushed home she went to her grandfather and repeated the trick how hurt she felt to see that only ink came out of the glass grandfather's clothes were spoiled to grandfather however, burst into laughter and hugged Suheena

J. Question Tags

The teacher was talking to the class about Anshu, who had made a beautiful painting. The teacher said, "She has made a beautiful painting, hasn't she? And almost everybody said, "Yes Ma'am, she has." When the teacher announced a prize for Anshu, Sneha said,

"We are proud of her, aren't we?"

"You haven't learnt painting in any school, have you?" the teacher asked Anshu. And Anshu said, "No, mam, I haven't."

Now look at these three sentences:

1. She has made a beautiful painting, hasn't she?
2. We are proud of her, aren't we?
3. You haven't learn painting in any school, have you?

Each of these sentences has two parts: a statement (She has made a beautiful painting) and a short question (hasn't she?). This short question has been tagged onto the statement, so it is called a question tag.

Why do we use question tags? In response to the question tag, hasn't she? The children say, "Yes mam, she has." It means that the children confirm what the teacher says.

Similarly, when the teacher says, "You have not learnt painting in any school, have you?" Anshu confirms that she hasn't.

- A question tag is a short question placed at the end of a statement, usually in informal English.
- A question tag is used to get a statement confirmed.

K.   How to Form Question Tags –1

She has made a beautiful painting, hasn't she?

- The question tag consists of only two words, hasn't she? It has the same subject as the statement (she). We can use a pronoun of the same person as the subject.
- If the main sentence has an auxiliary verb, the auxiliary verb is repeated in the question tag.

She hasn't learnt painting in any school, has she?
In the above statement the auxiliary *has* is used in both the parts.

- If the main sentence does not have any auxiliary verb, we use do, does, did in the question tag according to the tense. For example,

  He doesn't make a noise, does he?
  She didn't play badminton, did she?

- The tense remains the same. For example,

  She won the first prize in speech competition, didn't she?
  He left his home forever, didn't he?

- If the statement is positive, the question tag will be negative and if the statement is negative, the question tag will be positive. For example,

  We are proud of her, aren't we?
  You haven't hurt her, have you.

- In negative question tags we usually use short forms of the negatives: don't, won't, , didn't, haven't, ain't, shan't, etc.

  Let us take some more examples:
  A

1. Madhu is proud, isn't she?
2. You will give me your notes, won't you?
3. He learned painting in France didn't he?
4. Mukul drives smoothly, doesn't he?

  B

1. They cannot come so early, can they?
2. It is not fair to leave him behind, is it?
3. She does not tell lies, does she?
4. I don't owe you any money, do I?

Note:

We must not write such sentences as:

1. Madhu is proud, isn't it? Write: isn't she?
2. You will help me, isn't it? Write: won't you?

AX.   How to Form Question Tags—2

Basic questions in English are formed using the auxiliary verb followed by the subject which comes before the main verb.
Auxiliary Verb + Subject + Main Verb

- *Do you live in Poland?*
- *How long has she worked at that company?*

Sometimes we don't really want to ask a question but just want to check information. For example, if you are sure that a friend lives in Seattle but want to check to make sure, you might use a question tag.

- *Tom lives in Seattle, doesn't he?*

In this case, it isn't necessary to ask a question because you already know the information. Using a question tag helps you confirm that the information you know is correct. Question tags can also change meaning based on how you pronounce the tag at the end of the sentence. If you raise your voice on the question tag you are asking if the information you just stated is indeed correct. Using question tags in this manner helps to make sure that you are doing something correctly, or understand a situation accurately. Here are some examples:

- A mom buying some jeans for her daughter: *You wear size 2, don't you?*

- A friend writing a birthday card to a friend: *Peter was born on March 2, wasn't he?*
- A job interviewer checking information on a resume: *You haven't worked at this company before, have you?*

At other times, you drop the voice at the question tag. When dropping the voice at the question tag, you indicate that you are <u>confirming information</u>. Here are some examples:

- Young man filling out a form speaking to his wife: *We live on Cherry St, don't we?*
- Friend looking at a calendar with a meeting noted: *We're meeting later this afternoon, aren't we?*
- Friend speaking to her friend as they walk in the rain: *The sun won't shine today, will it?*

Forming question tags is very easy. Remember that the question tag uses the auxiliary verb in the opposite form of the sentence itself. In other words, if the sentence is positive, the question tag takes the negative form of the auxiliary verb. If the sentence is negative, the question tag employs the positive form. Here's a quick review of principle tenses, the auxiliary form they take, and an example of a positive and a negative question tag for each tense:

EXAMPLE 1.

Tense: <u>Past Continuous</u>

Auxiliary Verb: Was / Were (to be)

Positive Sentence Question Tag Example: Andy was working when you arrived, wasn't he?

Negative Sentence Question Tag Example: They weren't waiting for you, were they?

EXAMPLE 2.

Tense: Present Perfect

Auxiliary Verb: Have / Has (to have)

Positive Sentence Question Tag Example: Harry has lived in New York for a long time, hasn't he?

Negative Sentence Question Tag Example: We haven't visited our friends in Chicago this year, have we?

EXAMPLE 3.

Tense: Past Perfect

Auxiliary Verb: Had (to have)

Positive Sentence Question Tag Example: They had finished before he arrived, hadn't they?

Negative Sentence Question Tag Example: Jason hadn't already finished before you provided the update, had he?

EXAMPLE 4.

Tense: Future with Will

Auxiliary Verb: Will

Positive Sentence Question Tag Example: Tom will think about it, won't he?

Negative Sentence Question Tag Example: They won't be able to come to the party, will they?

EXAMPLE 5.

Tense: Future with Going to

Auxiliary Verb: Is / Are / Am (to be)

Positive Sentence Question Tag Example: Tom is going to study Russian, isn't he?

Negative Sentence Question Tag Example: They aren't going to be at the meeting, are they?

Do you know how to use question tags like *is he* and *didn't you*?

Look at these examples to see how question tags are used.

You haven't seen this film, have you?
Your sister lives in Spain, doesn't she?
He can't drive, can he?

We can add question tags like *isn't it?, can you?* or *didn't they?* to a statement to make it into a question. Question tags are more common in speaking than writing.

We often use question tags when we expect the listener to agree with our statement. In this case, when the statement is positive, we use a negative question tag.

She's a doctor, isn't she?
Yesterday was so much fun, wasn't it?

If the statement is negative, we use a positive question tag.

He isn't here, is he?
The trains are never on time, are they?
Nobody has called for me, have they?

If we are sure or almost sure that the listener will confirm that our statement is correct, we say the question tag with a falling intonation. If we are a bit less sure, we say the question tag with a rising intonation.

Formation

If there is an auxiliary verb in the statement, we use it to form the question tag.

I don't need to finish this today, do I?
James is working on that, isn't he?
Your parents have retired, haven't they?
The phone didn't ring, did it?
It was raining that day, wasn't it?
Your mum hadn't met him before, had she?

Sometimes there is no auxiliary verb already in the statement. For example, when:

... the verb in the statement is present simple or past simple and is positive. Here we use *don't, doesn't* or *didn't*:

Jenni eats cheese, doesn't she?
I said that already, didn't I?

... the verb in the statement is *to be* in the present simple or past simple. In this case we use *to be* to make the question tag:

The bus stop's over there, isn't it?
None of those customers were happy, were they?

... the verb in the statement is a modal verb. Here we use the modal verb to make the question tag:

They could hear me, couldn't they?
You won't tell anyone, will you?

If the main verb or auxiliary verb in the statement is *am*, the positive question tag is *am I?* but the negative question tag is usually *aren't I?*:

I'm never on time, am I?

I'm going to get an email with the details, aren't I?

A tag question is a special construction in English. It is a statement followed by a mini-question. We use tag questions to ask for confirmation. They mean something like: "Is that right?" or "Do you agree?" They are very common in English.

Notice:

- *won't* is the contracted form of *will not*
- the tag repeats the auxiliary verb, not the main verb. Except, of course, for the verb *be* in Present Simple and Past Simple.

Answering Tag Questions

How do we answer a tag question? Often, we just say *Yes* or *No*. Sometimes we may repeat the tag and reverse it (They don't live here, *do they*? Yes, *they do*). Be very careful about answering tag questions. In some languages, an opposite system of answering is used, and non-native English speakers sometimes answer in the wrong way. This can lead to a lot of confusion!

For example, everyone knows that snow is white. Look at these questions, and the correct answers:

In some languages, people answer a question like "Snow isn't black, is it?" with "Yes" (meaning "Yes, I agree with you"). This is the **wrong answer** in English!

Here are some more examples, with correct answers:

- The moon goes round the earth, doesn't it? Yes, it does.
- The earth is bigger than the moon, isn't it? Yes.
- The earth is bigger than the sun, isn't it? **No, it isn't!**
- Asian people don't like rice, do they? **Yes, they do!**
- Elephants live in Europe, don't they? **No, they don't!**
- Men don't have babies, do they? No.

- The English alphabet doesn't have 40 letters, does it? No, it doesn't.

Tag Question Special Cases

Negative adverbs

The adverbs *never, rarely, seldom, hardly, barely* and *scarcely* have a negative sense. Even though they may be in a positive statement, the feeling of the statement is negative. We treat statements with these words like negative statements, so the question tag is normally positive. Look at these examples:

Intonation

We can change the *meaning* of a tag question with the musical pitch of our voice. With rising intonation, it sounds like a real question. But if our intonation falls, it sounds more like a statement that doesn't require a real answer:

Imperatives

Sometimes we use question tags with imperatives (invitations, orders), but the sentence remains an imperative and does not require a direct answer. We use *won't* for invitations. We use *can, can't, will, would* for orders.

Same-way tag questions

Although the basic structure of tag questions is positive-negative or negative-positive, it is sometimes possible to use a positive-positive or negative-negative structure. We use same-way tag questions to express interest, surprise, anger etc, and not to make real questions.

Look at these positive-positive tag questions:

- So you're having a baby, are you? That's wonderful!
- She wants to marry him, does she? Some chance!
- So you think that's funny, do you? Think again.

Negative-negative tag questions usually sound rather hostile:

- So you don't like my looks, don't you? (British English)

Asking for information or help

Notice that we often use tag questions to ask for information or help, starting with a negative statement. This is quite a friendly/polite way of making a request. For example, instead of saying "Where is the police station?" (not very polite), or "Do you know where the police station is?" (slightly more polite), we could say: "You wouldn't know where the police station is, would you?" Here are some more examples:

- You don't know of any good jobs, do you?
- You couldn't help me with my homework, could you?
- You haven't got $10 to lend me, have you?

Mixed Examples of Tag Questions

Here is a list of examples of tag questions in different contexts. Notice that some are "normal" and others seem to break all the rules:

- But you don't really love her, do you?

- This'll work, won't it?
- Oh you think so, do you?
- Well, I couldn't help it, could I?
- But you'll tell me if she calls, won't you?
- We'd never have known, would we?
- Oh you do, do you?
- The weather's bad, isn't it?
- You won't be late, will you?
- Nobody knows, do they?
- You never come on time, do you?
- You couldn't help me, could you?
- You think you're clever, do you?
- So you don't think I can do it, don't you? (British English)
- Shut up, will you!
- She can hardly love him after all that, can she?
- Nothing will happen, will it?

ALL.   How to Form Question Tags –3

1.   I am

The question tag for *I am* is *aren't I?*
I am right, aren't I?

2.   Imperatives

a.   After positive commands, will you? and won't you? can both be used:

Please come in, won't you?
Post this letter on your way to the post office, won't you?

b.   After negative commands, we use will you?

Don't forget to wake me up, will you?

Don't try to hurt her, will you?

3. Let us

After let us, we use shall we?
Let us sit in the sun, shall we?
Let us wait for the rain to stop, shall we?
Let us hope for the best, shall we?
Let us face the music, shall we?
Question Tags

- Positive statement ....negative question tag
- Negative statement ....positive question tag
- No change of tense
- Auxiliary in a statement ...auxiliary repeated in the tag
- No auxiliary ...do/does/did in the tag
- I am ...the tag is: aren't I?
- Positive commands ...the tag is: will you/won't you
- Negative command ...the tag is: will you
- Let us ...the tag is: shall we

Exercise 10. Add appropriate question tags to the following statements:

1. Our Prime Minister is a man of great learning.
2. Roopam was present in the class yesterday.
3. After independence, India has progressed a lot.
4. He will make an excellent speech.
5. You usually attend all the classes.
6. Mrs Gupta, teaches both English and History.
7. Yesterday, the principal left the office early.
8. We must abide by all the rules.
9. He goes to school every day.
10. They want to have and honest servant.
11. She proved her mettle in all the fields.

12. He wanted to mess up with them.

Exercise 11. Add appropriate question tags to the following statements:

1. These children aren't naughty.
2. This job is not suitable for me.
3. She was not telling a lie.
4. She had not paid her dues yet.
5. We cannot park our car here.
6. You did not submit the assignment on time.
7. He will not deceive you.
8. They have not gone so far.
9. She does not know how to paint.
10. They will not pay the fee.
11. He did not commit that sin.
12. The child was not crying.

Exercise 12. Add appropriate question tags to the following statements:

1. You don't take sugar in your tea.
2. The army has an important role to play.
3. These fans are of superior quality.
4. This road doesn't lead to the railway station.
5. I am a bit early.
6. Have a cup of tea.
7. Please leave me alone.
8. Let us request the teacher to explain this poem again.
9. She doesn't play squash.
10. He is a bit nervous.
11. They don't follow the right path.
12. Karma has its own role to play in our life.

CHAPTER TWO

Nouns

A noun is the name of a person, animal, place, things, state or abstract ideas. In other words, everything that is visible and something which is not visible but can be sensed is called a noun. Nouns have been divided into four broad categories:

1. Proper Noun
2. Common Noun
3. Collective Noun
4. Abstract Noun

1. Proper Noun:

Proper nouns have two distinct features: They name specific one-of-a-kind items, and they begin with capital letters, no matter where they occur within a sentence. Here, we'll take a closer look at proper nouns, provide proper noun examples, and help you learn how to use a proper noun the right way. Remember that all <u>nouns</u> are words naming people, animals, places, things, and ideas. Every noun can be further classified as either common or proper. The distinction is very easy to make once you see some examples and come up with a few of your own.

Proper Noun Examples

In the following sentences, proper noun examples are compared with <u>common nouns</u>. Notice that the proper nouns are specific and unique, while the common nouns are much more general in nature.

1. *Common noun: I want to be a **writer**.*

   *Proper noun: **Agatha Christie** wrote many books.*

1. *Common noun: I'd like to adopt a **cat**.*

   *Proper noun: **Cleopatra** is the cutest kitten ever.*

3. *Common noun: Would you like a **cookie**?*

   *Proper noun: I'm craving **Oreos**.*

4. *Common noun: Let's go to the **city**.*

   *Proper noun: Let's go to **San Francisco**.*

5. *Common noun: My **teacher** starts work before sunup.*

   *Proper noun: **Mr. Bell** seems to understand what students need.*

6. *Common noun: I think that's a **planet**, not a **star**.*

   *Proper noun: I can see **Jupiter** tonight.*

7. *Common noun: He's always hanging out with his **girlfriend**.*

   *Proper noun: He never goes anywhere without **Sarah**.*

8. *Common noun: There are a lot of important **documents** in the archives.*

Proper noun*: There are many important documents at* ***The Library of Congress****.*

How to Use Proper Nouns

It's easy to use proper nouns, once you know what they are. Simply place them in your sentences as you would common nouns, ensuring that you capitalize them. Here are some examples to help you get started.

- Brett had hoped for an easy teacher for his algebra class, but he got Ms. Boggs, whose unreasonable demands and short temper made the semester unbearable.

  → *Teacher* is a common noun. *Ms. Boggs* is a proper noun.

- Gloria had a craving, and not just any cookie would do. She went to the store and bought a box of Oreos.

  → *Cookie* is a common noun. *Oreos* is a proper noun.

- We wanted to try a new restaurant, so we went to Taste of Thai.

  → *Restaurant* is a common noun. *Taste of Thai* is a proper noun.

Proper Noun Examples

Identify the proper noun in each sentence:

1. The boy threw the ball to his dog, Wilson.
2. I'd like you to meet my friend Jeremy.
3. We'll be vacationing in Aspen this year.
4. My second grade teacher was Mrs. Gilbert, an old battle-axe.
5. We went to Smith's Furniture and bought a new couch to replace our old one.

6. Do you think the Dolphins will win the game?
7. I'm flying first-class on Emirate Airlines.
8. Thomas Jefferson was a president and philosopher.
9. My best friend moved to Israel to study.
10. When the Titanic sank, the captain went down with the ship.

Answers: 1 – **Wilson**, 2 – **Jeremy**, 3 – **Aspen**, 4 – **Mrs. Gilbert**, 5 – **Smith's Furniture**, 6 – **Dolphins**, 7 – **Emirate Airlines**, 8 – **Thomas Jefferson**, 9 – **Israel**, 10 – **Titanic**

2. Common Noun

At some point, everyone has the same question: What is a common noun? Here, we'll take a look at common nouns and provide some common noun examples so you can easily recognize common nouns when you see them. Don't worry, this will be painless.

What is a Common Noun?

A <u>noun</u> is a word that names a person, animal, place, thing, or idea. All nouns can be further classified as a <u>proper</u> or common noun. Common nouns are words used to name general items rather than specific ones. Go into your living room. What do you see? A lamp, chair, couch, TV, window, painting, pillow, candle – all of these items are named using common nouns.

Common nouns are everywhere, and you use them all the time, even if you don't realize it. Wherever you go, you'll find at least one common noun. Street, closet, bathroom, school, mall, gas station, living room; all of these places are things, and thus they are common nouns.

What is the difference between common and proper nouns?

When we look at the two main types of noun – proper and common – we can differentiate between the two by saying that a common noun is a general way of classifying something, and a proper noun is a specific way of classifying something, So, for example, the word *dog* is a common noun; but if your dog was called Fido, the word *Fido* is a proper noun:

- **Dog** = common noun
- **Dog's name** (Fido, in this case) = proper noun

More examples of the difference between common and proper nouns:

- My favorite *newspaper* (common noun) is the *Washington Post* (proper noun).
- Her *husband* (common noun) is called *Frank* (proper noun).
- The award-winning **Babe Ruth** (proper noun) is the greatest *baseball player* (common noun) in history.

You may have noticed from the examples that common nouns are not usually capitalized, unless they begin a sentence, whereas proper nouns are normally capitalized. You will also notice that both types of nouns can be more than a single word.

When to use common nouns?

We use common nouns to denote a class of objects or a concept. Consider the word *star*, as in *the stars we see in the sky. Star* is used as a common noun, used to denote the class of objects that we view in the night sky, i.e. the luminescent bodies that are spread across the universe, twinkling overhead. *The Sun,* however, is a proper noun, used to describe the specific star that is at the center of our solar system.

So, anything that is a thing can be generally classified as a common noun:

Professions: *lawyer, doctor, teacher, nurse, politician, football player.*

People: People in general are named using common nouns, though their official titles in certain cases or given names are proper nouns. When we refer to people using common nouns, we use words like *teacher, clerk, police officer, preacher, delivery driver, boyfriend, girlfriend, grandma, cousin,* and *barista.*

For example, when talking about your *mother*, *mother* is a common noun.

- My *mother* is an actress.
- Barbara's *mother* was the best cook in the city.

But when speaking to your *mother*, or using *mother* as her name, *mother* is used as a proper noun.

- "*Mother*, can you bake your brownies for the party?"
- I asked *Mother Thompson* to join us at dinner.

Objects:*car, newspaper, boat, potato chip, shoe, house, table, sword.*

However, common nouns can also be more abstract concepts, not things but ideas, emotions and experiences, for example:

Abstract ideas: *Culture, love, democracy, time, hatred, peace, war, empathy, anger, laughter.*

How to recognize a common noun?

Considering what we have laid out above, it should be pretty easy to recognize a common noun. However, there are some cases when it can be tricky. Consider these sentences:

- *Queen Elizabeth II* welcomed *President Donald Trump* to *Buckingham Palace.*
- Donald Trump visited many *queens* and *palaces* during his tenure as the *president* of the United States.

In the first sentence, *Queen Elizabeth II, President Trump* and *Buckingham Palace* are proper nouns. They are specific titles for a specific person. In the second sentence, *queens, palaces* and *president* are common nouns. *Queens* and *palaces* refer to queens and palaces in general, and *president* refers to the job title and not the specific person.

We mentioned earlier that job titles and general titles fall under the category of common nouns – attorney, actor, comedian, truck driver, sergeant, officer, secretary. However, if these become specific titles referring to a specific person, they sometimes become proper nouns as in the examples above. Normally, this means the words are capitalized when placed directly in front of that person's name:

- *Attorney General* William Barr was appointed by *President*

But look how we can use the same words with common nouns:

- Each US president must appoint an attorney general while in office.

So, you can recognize the common noun by the fact it is not capitalized. But remember that common nouns can also be identified because they are referring to non-specific things or classifications.

The takeaway is this: common nouns are general names and unless they are part of a title like *Postmaster General* or begin a sentence, they're not usually capitalized.

Common Noun Examples

The following common noun examples will help you to recognize common nouns. In the sentences that follow, common noun examples are italicized. Notice that the examples providing proper nouns name specific versions of the same type of person, animal, place, thing, or idea.

1. *Common Noun*: You broke my favorite *mug*. *Proper Noun*: I can't believe you broke my *Snoopy mug*.
2. *Common Noun*: I really want a new pair of *jeans*. *Proper Noun*: I really want to buy a new pair of *Levis*.
3. *Common Noun*: I wish I could remember the name of that *painter*. *Proper Noun*: I really love art by *Van Gogh*.
4. *Common Noun*: They're all waiting for us at the *restaurant*. *Proper Noun*: Everyone else is at *Bill's Burgers*.
5. *Common Noun*: I really want to live in the *city Proper Noun*: Of all the places I've lived, *Denver* was best.
6. *Common Noun*: Let's go to watch a live game at the *stadium*. *Proper Noun*: Let's try to get good seats at *Wrigley Field*

Countables and Uncountables

Nouns like country, city, river, person, class, books can be counted. So, they are called countables or countable nouns. Generally speaking, most of the common and collective nouns are countables.

Proper nouns like India, Kapil, Kanpur, or any particular names of person, place or things. There is only one of their kind. So, they are called uncountable nouns. Some of the material nouns are uncountable; things which we cannot count but only measure are uncountables. For example, wood, milk, tea, ink, glass, gold, copper, silver, etc.

Abstract nouns like kindness, honesty, faithfulness, bitterness, sweetness, etc. cannot be measured and are called uncountables too.

However, in certain cases, abstract nouns may also have a plural form: memories, pleasures, decisions, hardships, vacancies, etc.

Soap is an uncountable but we may have cakes of soap. Paper is also uncountable but we can have sheets of paper. Wheat, rice, money and the likes are uncountables.

Some words can be used both as a countable and an uncountable:

These houses are made of stones. (Stone is an uncountable)

The child threw a stone at me. (Stone is countable here)

A countable noun has a plural form; an uncountable does not have one.

For example, we can think of dogs, trees, mountains, classes, armies but we cannot think of kindnesses, prides, loves, etc.

The jug is made of glass. (Gass is uncountable)

I have taken three glasses of water. (Glass is countable)

I don't like tea. (Tea is uncountable)

Ihe has for cups of tea. (Tea is countable)

Countable may be used with such words as a, one, two, few, a few, many, etc.

A pen, one student, a few apples, many children.

Uncountables cannot be used with these words. We cannot say a milk, a tea, an ink, one wheat, few kindness, etc. With uncountables, we can use words like little, much, less, etc.

For example, a little milk, much help, etc.

Exercise 1. Underline the nouns in the following story and indicate what kind of noun they are:

The great Alexander works visited the studio of a sculptor in Athens. The studio was full of statues, one of which looked rather strange. Its face was covered and there were wings on the feet. "What statue is this?" asked Alexander. "It represents opportunity.", said the sculptor. "The covered face means that people are not able to recognise an opportunity when it approaches. Its wings suggests that it moves off at a greatest speed, and once it is gone, it does not come back."

Alexander was greatly impressed. He said, "You are really a great artist. You have shown me not only beauty but wisdom also. I too have always believed that grabbing an opportunity and using it to our advantage is the key to success."

Formation of Abstract Nouns

We can form abstract nouns

1. From adjectives:

Brave---bravery; long----length false----falsehood.

2. From verbs:

Know---knowledge; choose---choice; judge---judgement.

3. From common nouns:

Child---childhood; friend---friendship; slave---slavery.

Let us learn how abstract nouns are formed with the help of some common suffixes. Note that in certain cases when a suffix is added to a word, we may have to alter spellings slightly.

Suffix
Word
Abstract noun
acy
private
privacy
age
break
breakage
short
shortage
marry
marriage
al
arrive
arrival
dismiss
dissmal
ance
assist
assistant
dom
free

freedom
ence
absent
absence
innocent
innocence
patient
patience
hood
boy
boyhood
child
childhood
ity
equal
equality
moral
morality
real
reality
timid
timidity
active
activity
clear
clarity
generous
generosity
noble
nobility
ice
coward
cowardice
ment
agree

agreement
merry
merriment
pay
payment
treat
treatment
ness
blind
blindness
hard
hardness
holy
holiness
ship
friend
friendship
scholar
scholarship
hard
hardship
sion
decide
decision
omit
omission
th
bcar
birth
deep
depth
grow
growth
long
length

true
truth
young
youth
tion
act
action
invent
invention
protect
protection
destroy
destruction
imagine
imagination
invite
invitation
repeat
repetition
ty
certain
certainty
loyal
loyalty
y
discover
discovery
honest
honesty
unite
unity
others
advise
advice
bind

bond
choose
choice
do
deed
feed
food
fly
flight
go
gait
high
height
know
knowledge
lend
loan
lose
loss
practise
practice
prove
proof
shake
shock
strike
stroke
weigh
weight
Some words are made into abstract noun in the following way:
Word
Abstract Noun
pass
passage
carry

carriage
waste
wastage
bury
burial
try
trial
abound
abundance
wise
wisdom
excellent
excellence
obedient
obedience
present
presence
child
childhood
man
manhood
human
humanity
popular
popularity
stupid
stupidity
able
ability
brief
brevity
curious
curiosity
necessary
necessity

stable
stability
just
justice
appoint
appointment
move
movement
punish
punishment
cheap
cheapness
large
largeness
hard
hardship
invade
invasion
provide
provision
broad
breadth
die
death
heal
health
strong
strength
wide
width
attract
attraction
perfect
perfection
deceive

deception
educate
education
introduce
introduction
receive
reception
cruel
cruelty
anxious
anxiety
flatter
flattery
modest
modesty
believe
belief
brave
bravery
depart
departure
fail
failure
flow
flood
give
gift
hate
hatred
hot
heat
laugh
laughter
live
life

please
pleasure
proud
prides
see
sight
sit
seat
speak
speech
think
thought

Exercise 2. Make abstract nouns from the following words by adding one of these suffixes: ment, ness, th, ity:

fair
grow
quick
busy
pure
argue
agree
popular
long
dark
true
merry
brief
clear
heavy
heal
noble
treat
judge

bear

Exercise 3. Make abstract nouns from the following words by adding one of these suffixes: ance, ence, hood, tion, dom:

child

innocent

appear

repeat

brilliant

assist

free

false

boy

present

protect

act

ignorant

starve

wise

Exercise 4. Fill in the blanks with the noun form of the words given in the brackets:

1. An.............................was signed between the landlord and the tenant. (agree)
2. The spectators burst into ....at the ....of the clown. (laugh, see)
3. Chandragupta Vikramaditya is famous for his .... (just)
4. The factory faced an acute .... of raw material. (short)
5. There is no .... in this office. (vacant)
6. She listened to the whole story with great .... (patient)
7. After the wedding, they gave a grand .... (receive)
8. The country cannot progress unless there is .... among the citizens. (unite)

9. .... can be achieved only through .... (perfect, practise)

Collective Nouns

Collective nouns can be a little tricky to identify and use. Are they singular, or are they plural? What type of verb do I use with a collective noun? With a little practice, collective nouns can quickly be mastered.

In this post we'll review what collective nouns are, the singular and plural forms of collective nouns, and how to ensure proper subject-verb agreement when using collective nouns.

What is a Collective Noun?

A collective noun is a word or phrase that represents a group of people or things but is treated as a singular entity (Hint: a "collection" of people or things). Even though you can count the individual members of the group, you usually think of the individuals as a group, a whole, or as one unit.

Because collective nouns describe a plurality of something, they are often confused with plural nouns. Additionally, collective nouns can be made into plural nouns, like most common nouns.

Consider this: A group is learning about different types of nouns.

There are three nouns in the sentence above. One is a collective noun, and the others are plural nouns.

Collective Noun: group

Plural Nouns: types, nouns

What is the relationship between collective and plural nouns?

Plural means more than one, so plural nouns are referring to more than one of that particular noun. The most common way to make a noun plural is by adding an 's' to the end of the word, though there are various reals related to making singular nouns plural.

Examples:

Singular: Tree / Plural: Trees

Singular: Student / Plural: Students

Collective nouns are singular words used in place of plural nouns. Collective nouns can be singular or plural, but plural nouns are always plural.

Let's use the example from above: A group is learning about different types of nouns.

What is a group? It is a collection of people, places, or things. In this case, we can infer that the group is a number of students.

The word "students" is a plural noun for student.

The sentence could be written without using a collective noun: Students are learning about different types of nouns.

So aren't collective nouns plural if they are made up of more than one of the same thing? It's easy to make the mistake of thinking collective nouns are plural; however, these words are designed to represent a single unit of more than one of the same thing.

Collective nouns can also be plural: Groups are learning about different types of nouns.

What does "groups" mean in this sentence? It means more than one group, making it a plural collective noun.

Collective Proper Nouns

Collective nouns may also be proper nouns when that proper noun represents a group.

- Music groups and businesses are often used as collective nouns.

  - Maroon 5 is playing on the radio.

    - Since Maroon 5 is a music group with multiple members, it is a collective proper noun, and It is treated as a singular noun in a sentence.

- Target is a popular store for everyday needs.

  - Since Target is a large retail chain, it would be considered a collective proper noun in this sentence.
  - If a specific Target is being referenced, it is no longer being used as a collective proper noun, and is treated as a singular proper noun in a sentence.

    - I shop at the Target on the corner.

- Hint: If you substitute a generic collective noun like "the band" or "the company" with the proper noun, you can see that the proper noun is a collective noun, so it should be treated as a collective noun in a sentence with singular verbs.

Some collective proper nouns, sports teams in particular, often use the plural form of the team name and require the use of a plural verb and plural pronouns as needed:

- The Cubs have won the World Series, breaking their 107 year losing streak.

However, if the name of a city is used in place of the team name, it is treated as a singular noun:

- Chicago won the World Series, breaking its 107 year losing streak.

How do you use collective nouns?

Collective nouns can be used in any type of sentence, but the most common mistakes made when using collective nouns is subject-verb disagreement and pronoun disagreement.

Subject-Verb Agreement:

If a singular collective noun is used in a sentence, it needs to be treated like a singular noun.

Incorrect Example: The team are playing in the championship game.

Correct Example: The team is playing in the championship game.

We use the singular verb "is" with a collective noun, because a collective noun represents a singular unit. If the collective noun is made plural, than the verb will follow plural noun rules:

The teams are playing in the championship game.

Let's look again at our sample sentences and add one more using a singular noun for students:

1. A group is learning about different types of nouns.
2. Students are learning about different types of nouns.
3. Groups are learning about different types of nouns.
4. A Student is learning about different types of nouns.

What differences do you see in the sentences?

1. A group is learning about different types of nouns.
2. Students **are** learning about different types of nouns.
3. Groups **are** learning about different types of nouns.
4. **A** student **is** learning about different types of nouns.

You'll notice that verb usage for singular nouns are the same. Sentences 1 and 4 use the singular verb "is".

The sentences with singular nouns also use the article "A" before the noun.

The verb usage for plural nouns are the same as well. Sentences 2 and 3 use the plural verb "are", and there is no need for an article before the noun.

Subject-Pronoun Agreement

Pronoun agreement follows the same rules as verb agreement for collective nouns. Singular pronouns are used for singular collective nouns, and plural pronouns are used for plural collective nouns.

Incorrect Example: The bouquet of flowers is wilting, even though they were labeled as fresh.

Correct Example: The bouquet of flowers is wilting, even though it was labeled as fresh.

We use the singular pronoun "it" with a collective noun, because a collective noun represents a singular unit. If the collective noun is made plural, than the pronoun will follow plural noun rules:

The bouquets of flowers are wilting, even though they were labeled as fresh.

3 Tips For Recognizing and Using Collective Nouns

Tip #1: If it takes more than one person, animal, or thing to use the word, it's probably a collective noun

- Remember: Collective nouns are words or phrases that represent a group of people or things as a singular unit.

  - Think: If I was looking at a flock flying across the sky, would I be seeing one thing, or multiple things together?

    - If I was looking at a flock, I would be looking at a group of birds flying together. So flock is a collective noun.

Tip #2. Subject-Verb Agreement. Singular collective nouns use singular verbs, plural collective nouns use plural verbs

- Remember: Collective nouns are considered singular unless it is specifically made plural. Verbs used with collective nouns need to follow proper subject-verb agreement by using singular verbs with singular collective nouns, and plural verbs only when the collective noun has been made plural.

- The class is expected to follow classroom expectations.
- The classes are expected to follow classroom expectations.

Tip #3: Pronoun Agreement: Singular collective nouns use singular pronouns, plural collective nouns use plural pronouns

- Remember: Just like subject-verb agreement, pronoun agreement needs to be carefully checked to make sure singular pronouns are used for singular collective nouns, and plural pronouns are used for plural collective nouns.

  - The crew on the aircraft carrier is prepared to deploy if it is called on.
  - The crews on the aircraft carriers are prepared to deploy if they are called on.

Applying the Basics: Collective Noun Practice

Now that you understand *what* collective nouns are, and *how* to use them properly in a sentence, let's practice identifying them and checking for proper verb and pronoun usage. Remember, collective nouns are considered singular nouns, and they should be used with singular verbs and pronouns.

The Ultimate List of Collective Nouns

Refer to the chart below for an extensive list of common collective nouns.

Collective Nouns: Identifying Collective Nouns

Complete the quick exercise below to assess your mastery of collective nouns.

Select the collective noun(s) in the sentences below. Remember, a collective noun is a word or phrase that represents a group of people or things but is treated as a singular entity. Collective nouns can be made plural like most common nouns.

1. I went with a group of students to see the statues commemorating the army of soldiers that fought in the Korean War.

- In this sentence, *group* and *army* are collective nouns. Each word represents multiple people in a single unit.

2. The audience cheered as the team took the field for the first game in the series against its biggest rival.

- In this sentence, *audience*, *team*, and *series* are collective nouns. Each word represents multiple people or things in a single unit.

3. The committees are working on different projects to help increase community involvement in school events.

- In this sentence, *committees* and *community* are collective nouns. The word *committees* is also a plural collective noun. Each word represents multiple people in a single unit or units.

4. His family bought a bunch of movies from Best Buy to donate to the company's gift drive.

- In this sentence, *family*, *bunch*, *Best Buy*, and *company's* are collective nouns. *Best Buy* is a proper collective noun, and *company's* has an apostrophe and an 's', because it is also acting as a possessive noun. Each word or phrase represents multiple people or things in a single unit.

5. The Students wishing to start a school choir met with the school board and faculty to present a list of arguments supporting the idea.

- In this sentence, *choir, board, faculty*, and *list* are collective nouns. Each word represents multiple people or things in a single unit.

Pro tip: When evaluating whether a noun is a collective noun, ask yourself, "Does this word represent multiple people or things as one unit?"

Collective Nouns: Identifying Subject-Verb Agreement and Disagreement

Complete the quick exercise below to assess your mastery of subject-verb agreement when using collective nouns.

Review each sentence and select the verb that ensures accurate subject-verb agreement. Remember, a collective noun is a singular noun and uses singular verbs. Collective nouns can be made plural and use plural verbs.

1. The mob of Black Friday shoppers (is, are) anxiously waiting for the store to open.

- The correct verb for this sentence is *is*, because the subject, mob, is a singular collective noun.

2. His Science class (take, takes) the AP® exam on Friday.

- The correct verb for this sentence is *takes*, because the subject, class, is a singular collective noun.

3. On Saturday, the local girl scout troops (sell, sells) cookies outside of the grocery stores.

- The correct verb for this sentence is *sell*, because the subject, troops, is a plural collective noun.

4. The congregation (sings, sing) the hymn along with the pastor.

- The correct verb for this sentence is *sings*, because the subject, congregation, is a singular collective noun.

5. The apple orchard I go to every fall (have, has) 30 varieties of apples and the best brunch around.

- The correct verb for this sentence is *has*, because the subject, orchard, is a singular collective noun.

Pro tip: When evaluating whether or not a sentence has proper subject-verb agreement when the subject is a collective noun, ask yourself, "Is this collective noun singular or plural?" Singular collective nouns use singular verbs, and plural collective nouns use plural verbs. If you can replace the collective noun with the word "it", it is singular.

Collective Nouns: Identifying Subject-Pronoun Agreement and Disagreement

Complete the quick exercise below to assess your mastery of subject-pronoun agreement when using collective nouns.

Review each sentence and select the pronoun that ensures accurate subject-pronoun agreement. Remember, a collective noun is a singular noun and uses singular pronouns. Collective nouns can be made plural and use plural pronouns.

1. The staff was commended for (its, their) hard work this year.

- The correct pronoun for this sentence is *its*, because the subject, staff, is a singular collective noun.

2. Most people order a batch of chocolate chip cookies, because (it's, they're) the most popular item.

- The correct pronoun for this sentence is *it's*, the contraction 'it is', because the subject, batch, is a singular collective noun.

3. In the fall, I like to watch the flocks of birds flying south to (its, their) winter home.

- The correct pronoun for this sentence is *their*, because the subject, flocks, is a plural collective noun.

4. The lovely bouquet of roses smells like (it, they) came fresh from the garden.

- The correct pronoun for this sentence is *it*, because the subject, bouquet, is a singular collective noun.

5. The jury struggles to agree on a verdict, so (it, they) asks for more time to deliberate.

- The correct pronoun for this sentence is *it*, because the subject, jury, is a singular collective noun.

Pro tip: When evaluating whether or not a sentence has proper subject-pronoun agreement when the subject is a collective noun, ask yourself, "Is this collective noun singular or plural?" Singular collective nouns use singular pronouns, and plural collective nouns use plural pronouns. If you can replace the collective noun with the word "it", it is singular.

Common Group Names

Group Name "Herd"
Collective noun examples:

- *A herd of antelope*
- *A herd of boar*
- *A herd of buffaloes*
- *A herd of caribou*
- *A herd of cattle*

- *A herd of chamois*
- *A herd of chinchillas*
- *A herd of cows*
- *A herd of cranes*
- *A herd of deer*
- *A herd of donkeys*
- *A herd of elephants*
- *A herd of elk*
- *A herd of fairies*
- *A herd of giraffes*
- *A herd of gnus*
- *A herd of goats*
- *A herd of horses*
- *A herd of llamas*
- *A herd of moose*
- *A herd of oxen*
- *A herd of pigs*
- *A herd of ponies*
- *A herd of sea horses*
- *A herd of seals*
- *A herd of swans*
- *A herd of swine*
- *A herd of walruses*
- *A herd of whales*
- *A herd of wolves*
- *A herd of wrens*
- *A herd of yaks*
- *A herd of zebras*

Group Name "Pack"
Collective nouns list:

- *A pack of bears (polar bears)*
- *A pack of coyotes*
- *A pack of dogs*

- *A pack of grouse*
- *A pack of gulls*
- *A pack of hounds*
- *A pack of mongooses*
- *A pack of mules*
- *A pack of rats*
- *A pack of sharks*
- *A pack of stoats*
- *A pack of weasels*
- *A pack of wolves*

Group Name "Flock"
Collective nouns list:

- *A flock of birds*
- *A flock of bustards*
- *A flock of camels*
- *A flock of chickens*
- *A flock of ducks*
- *A flock of geese*
- *A flock of goats*
- *A flock of parrots*
- *A flock of pigeons*
- *A flock of seagulls*
- *A flock of sheep*
- *A flock of swifts*
- *A flock of tourists*
- *A flock of turkeys*

Group Name "Swarm"
Collective nouns list:

- *A swarm of ants*
- *A swarm of bees*
- *A swarm of butterflies*

- *A swarm of eels*
- *A swarm of flies*
- *A swarm of gnats*
- *A swarm of insects*
- *A swarm of rats*

Group Name "Shoal"
Collective noun examples:

- *A shoal of bass*
- *A shoal of fish*
- *A shoal of herrings*
- *A shoal of pilchards*
- *A shoal of salmon*

Group Name "Group"
Collective nouns list:

- *A group of guinea pigs*
- *A group of islands*
- *A group of people*
- *A group of dancers*
- *A group of engineers*

Group Name "Crowd"
Collective noun examples:

- *A crowd of onlookers*
- *A crowd of people*

Group Name "Gang"
Collective nouns list:

- *A gang of hoodlums*
- *A gang of laborers*

- *A gang of slaves*
- *A gang of thieves*
- *A gang of criminals*
- *A gang of crooks*
- *A gang of hoodlums*
- *A gang of prisoners*

Group Name "Mob"
Collective nouns list:

- *A mob of emus*
- *A mob of kangaroos*
- *A mob of meerkats*
- *A mob of thieves*
- *A mob of sheep*
- *A mob of kangaroos*
- *A mob of rioters*

Group Name "Staff"
Group names examples:

- *A staff of employees*
- *A staff of servants*

Group Name "Crew"
Group names examples:

- *A crew of sailors*

Group Name "Choir"
Group names examples:

- *A choir of angels*

Group Name "Orchestra"

Group names examples:

- *An orchestra of musicians*

Group Name "Panel"
Group names examples:

- *A panel of experts*

Group Name "Board"
Group names examples:

- *A board of directors*
- *A board of trustees*
- *A board of chess players*

Group Name "Troupe"
Collective nouns list:

- *A troupe of monkeys*
- *A troupe of shrimp*
- *A troupe of dancers*
- *A troupe of minstrels*
- *A troupe of performers*

Group Name "Bunch"
Group names examples:

- *A bunch of seals*
- *A bunch of pigeons*

Group Name "Pile"
Group names examples:

- *A pile of books*

Group Name "Heap"
Group names examples:

- *A heap of trash*

Group Name "Set"
Group names examples:

- *A set of bowls*
- *A set of utensils*

Group Name "Stack"
Group names examples:

- *A stack of books*

Group Name "Series"
Group names examples:

- *A series of events*
- *A series of photos*

Group Name "Shower"
Group names examples:

- *A shower of bastards*

Group Name "Fall"
Group names examples:

- *A fall of lambs*
- *A fall of woodcock*

List of collective nouns for people in English.

- A circle of friends
- A class of pupils
- A horde of savages
- A host of angels
- A house of senators
- A joint of osteopaths
- A lie/An equivocation of politicians
- A line of kings/rulers
- A melody of harpists
- A mess/An execution of officers
- A meter of percussionists
- A mob of rioters
- A morbidity of majors
- A mug/A reflection of narcissists
- A multiply/An unhappiness of husbands
- A mutter of mothers-in-law
- A wisdom of grandparents
- A number/A set of mathematicians
- A pack of Brownies
- A pack of thieves
- A pan of reviewers
- A panel of experts
- A party of friends
- A patrol of policemen
- A peck of Frenchmen
- A picket of strikers
- A pint of Irishmen
- A pity/A gang of prisoners
- A plush/A rascal of boys
- A pomposity of professors
- A posse of police
- A posse of sheriffs
- A pound of Englishmen
- A promise of barmen
- A prudence of vicars

- A quiz of teachers
- A rage of maidens
- A rash of dermatologists
- A regiment of soldiers
- A rookery/A school of clerks
- A rout of schoolboys
- A sample of salesmen
- A school of clerks
- A scolding of seamstresses
- A scoop/A slant of journalists
- A sentence of judges
- A series of radiologists
- A set/A subtlety of designers
- A set/A swish of hairdressers
- A shower of bastards
- A shower of meteorologists
- A shrivel of critics
- A shuffle of bureaucrats
- A side of dancers
- A simplicity of subalterns
- A poverty of pipers
- A slate of candidates
- A slither of gossip columnists
- A slouch of models
- A sneer of butlers
- A sprig of vegetarians
- A squad of beaters
- A squad of soldiers
- A squat of daubers
- A squeal of nieces
- A staff of employees
- A staff of servants
- A staff of teachers
- A stalk of foresters
- A subtlety of sergeants at law

- A superfluity of nuns
- A tabernacle of bakers
- A talent of gamblers
- A tantrum of decorators
- A team of athletes
- A team of players
- A thought of barons
- A tribe of Indians
- A tribe of natives
- A trip of hippies
- A troop of boy scouts
- A troupe of acrobats
- A troupe of artistes
- A troupe of dancers
- A troupe of performers
- A wandering of tinkers
- A wheeze of joggers
- A worship of writers
- An absence/An order of waiters
- An alley/A pratfall of clowns
- A brace/A wince of dentists
- An amalgamation of metallurgists
- An amble of walkers
- An ambush of widows
- An army of soldiers
- A roll of drummers
- An attitude/A grunt of teenagers
- An audience of listeners
- An eloquence of lawyers
- An embarrassment /A persistence of parents
- An entrance of actresses
- An expectation of heirs
- An expectation of midwives
- An obscurity/A rhyme of poets
- An illusion of magicians

- An impatience of wives
- An imposition of in-laws
- An obeisance of servants
- An observance of hermits
- An obstruction of dons

List of Collective Nouns for Birds

- A cloud of seafowls
- A colony/A flock/A raft of auks
- A colony of avocets
- A colony of gulls
- A colony of ibises
- A colony/A parcel/A rookery of penguins
- A covey/A brace/A brood/A flight/A pack of grouse
- A covey/A bevy/A clutch/A warren of partridges
- A covey of ptarmigans
- A crowd of redwings
- A descent of woodpeckers
- A desert/A deceit of lapwings
- A fall/A covey/A flight/A plump of woodcocks
- A flight of birds
- A flight/A gulp of cormorants
- A flight of goshawks
- A flight/A flock/A kit/A passel of pigeons
- A flight/A gulp of swallows
- A fling of dunlins
- A fling of sandpipers
- A flock of birds
- A flock of bustards
- A flock of swifts
- A flock of turkeys
- A flush of ducks
- A head/A herd of curlews
- A herd/A flock of wrens

- A hill of ruffs
- A host/A quarrel/A tribe/A ubiquity of sparrows
- A murder/A hover/A muster/A parcel of crows
- A chattering/A cloud/A congregation/A clutter of starlings
- A muse of capons
- A muster/An ostentation/A pride of peacocks
- A mustering/A flight/A phalanx of storks
- A mutation of thrushes
- A bouquet/A head/A warren of pheasants
- A parcel of linnets
- A parliament/A stare of owls
- A pitying of turtledoves
- A plump of moorhens
- A plump/A bunch/A knob/A raft of waterfowls
- A pod/A scoop of pelicans
- A prattle of parrots
- A pride/A flock of ostriches
- A rafter of turkeys
- A run of poultry
- A sedge/A siege of bitterns
- A sedge/A herd/A sedge/A siege of cranes
- A sedge/A flight/A hedge/A rookery/A siege of herons
- A flush/A puddling of mallards
- A spring/A bunch/A coil/A knob/A raft of teals
- A squabble of seagulls
- A stand of flamingos
- A trip of dotterels
- A trip/A bunch/A knob/A lute/A skein of wildfowls
- A wake of buzzards
- A walk/A wisp of snipes
- ...

List of Collective Nouns for Mammals

- A glaring/A cluster/A clutter of cats

- A cluster/A herd/A tribe of antelopes
- A coalition of cheetahs
- A cohort/A herd/A zeal of zebras
- A colony/A family/A lodge of beavers
- A colony of chinchillas
- A colony/A horde/A mischief/A swarm of rats
- A colony of voles
- A congress/A flange/A troop of baboons
- A coterie/A town of prairie dogs
- A couple of impalas
- A cowardice of curs
- A crash/A herd/A stubbornness of rhinoceroses
- A destruction of (wild) cats
- A destruction of wildcats
- A drift/A trip of (tame) swine
- A dray/A colony of squirrels
- A drift/A drove/A parcel of hogs
- A drove of bullocks
- A drove/A drift/A flock/A herd of pigs
- A drove/A herd of swine
- A fall of lambs
- A family/A bevy/A raft/A romp of otters
- A farrow/A litter of piglets
- A field/A string of racehorses
- A gang/A herb/An obstinacy of buffalos
- A gang/A herd of elks
- A grind of bottle-nosed whales
- A group of guinea pigs
- A herd/A gang of bisons
- A herd/A leash of bucks
- A herd of caribous
- A herd/A drift/A drove/A mob of cattle
- A herd of chamois
- A herd/A drove of donkeys
- A herd of elands

- A herd/A parade of elephants
- A herd/An implausibility of gnus
- A herd of hartebeests
- A herd of harts
- A herd of ibexes
- A herd of llamas
- A herd of moose
- A herd of wildebeests
- A herd of yaks
- A horde of gerbils
- A horde of hamsters
- A huddle/A herd/An ugly of walruses
- A husk of jackrabbits
- A journey/A group/A herd/A tower of giraffes
- A kindle/A litter of kittens
- A kindle of leverets
- A labor/A company/A movement of moles
- A leap of leopards
- A leash of greyhounds
- A litter of cubs
- A litter of pups
- A mischief/A horde/A nest/A trip of mice
- A mob/A troop of kangaroos
- A mob of wombats
- A nursery/A gaze of raccoons
- A pace/A drove/A coffle/A herd of asses
- A pack/A band/A rout of coyotes
- A pack/A kennel of dogs
- A pack/A trip of stoats
- A pack/A herd/A rout of wolves
- A parcel of hinds
- A pod/A flock/A school/A team of dolphins
- A prickle of porcupines
- A pride/A flock/A sault/A troop of lions
- A rake/A rack/A rag of colts

- A richness of martens
- A school/A herd/A pod of porpoises
- A shrewdness/A troop of apes
- A skulk/An earth/A lead/A leash/A troop of foxes
- A sloth of bears
- A sneak/A gang/A pack of weasels
- A sounder of (wild) boars
- A sounder of (wild) pigs

List of Collective Nouns for Sea Animals

- A glide of flying fish
- A glint/A troubling of goldfish
- A grind of blackfish
- A herd of seahorses
- A pack of perch
- A party of rainbow fish
- A quantity of smelts
- A school of butterfly fish
- A school of cod
- A shiver/A school/A shoal of sharks
- A shoal/A catch/A draught/A fray/A haul/A run/A school of fish
- A shoal of mackerel
- A shoal/A steam/A stream/A swarm of minnows
- A shoal/A school of pilchards
- A shoal of roach
- A shoal of shads
- A shoal/A spread of sticklebacks
- A squad of squid
- A swarm of dragonet fish
- A swarm of eels
- A troop of dogfish
- A troupe of shrimp
- ...

List of Collective Nouns for Insects

- A colony/An army/A bike/A swarm of ants
- A swarm/A bike/A cast/A cluster/A drift/A game/A hive/A stand/A rabble/A grist of bees
- A bike of (wild) bees
- A flight/A rabble/A swarm of butterflies
- An army of caterpillars
- An intrusion of cockroaches
- A swarm/A cloud/A business/A grist/A hatch of flies
- A cloud/A cluster/A swarm of grasshoppers
- A bike/A nest/A swarm of hornets
- A flight/A horde/A plague/A rabble/A swarm of insects
- A flock/A colony/An infestation of lice
- A plague/A cloud/A swarm of locusts
- A scourge/A swarm of mosquitoes
- A clutter/A cluster of spiders

List of <u>collective nouns for things</u> in English.

- A piece of jewellery
- A pile of money
- A drop of rain
- A ray of sunshine
- A pinch of salt
- A bar of soap
- A tube of toothpaste
- A ball of wool
- A bar of soap
- A battery of tests
- A bolt of lightning
- A bunch of books
- A bunch of keys
- A bunch of keys
- A chest of drawers

- A clump of reeds
- A deck of cards
- A fleet of ships
- A fleet of vehicles
- A flight of stairs
- A gallon of gasoline
- A group of friends
- A group of islands
- A grove of trees
- A hedge of bushes
- A library of books
- A pack of cards
- A pair of shoes
- A piece of furniture
- A piece of paper
- A quiver of arrows
- A ream of paper
- A roll of film/cloth
- A series of events
- A set of books
- A set of tools
- A shelf of books
- A stack of chairs
- A suite of furniture
- A suite of rooms

List of <u>collective nouns for food and drinks</u> in English.

- *A bar/A square of chocolate*
- *A batch of cakes*
- *A bottle of milk*
- *A bowl of rice*
- *A box of cereal*
- *A can of soda*
- *A carton of milk*

- *A cup of tea*
- *A glass of water*
- *A jar of honey*
- *A jug of water*
- *A kilo of meat*
- *A kilo of sugar*
- *A loaf of bread*
- *A packet of tea*
- *A piece of cheese*
- *A piece of chocolate*
- *A pile of cookies*
- *A slice of bread*
- *A slice of pizza*
- *A tub of margarine*

Exercise 1. Fill in the blanks with suitable **Collective Nouns:**

1. The cat has a .... of five kittens.

2. The .... of singers sang melodiously.

3. The jungle safari gave us an opportunity to spot a .... of lions.

4. The poachers were attacked by a .... of wild elephants.

5. A .... of bees forced us to take shelter in the cave.

6. A .... of stairs leads to the terrace.

7. The .... of musicians delivered a magical performance.

8. The children were amused by the .... of monkeys in the park.

9. A .... of grapes was hanging from the vine.

Exercise 2. Read the following sentences and underline the collective nouns.

1. The captain guided the team to play better.
2. The flock of sheep was grazing in the fields.
3. My father brought a bouquet of lilies for my mother.

4. The pack of wolves howled in the night.
5. A swarm of bees flew into the garden.
6. The hunter carries a quiver of arrows.
7. Our cat gave birth to a litter of kittens.
8. The army marched forward on the battlefield.
9. Can you pass me the bunch of keys?
10. The French destroyed the Armenian fleet.
11. Do you know about the cast of this movie?
12. The crew struggled to lead the ship past the stormy waves.
13. The board decided to appoint Riya as the Manager.
14. Please clean the pile of garbage.
15. The entire medical staff got infected by the Coronavirus.
16. The Beatles is a famous band.
17. The troupe performed the Macbeth drama.
18. The Andaman and Nicobar Islands comprises a group of 573 islands.
19. The jury passed a unanimous decision.
20. A cloud of dust swirled up during the storm.

Exercise 3. Fill in the blanks given in the following sentences with suitable collective nouns.

1. A number of people listening to a lecture/concert are called an______.
2. A group of people who sing in the church or public platforms is called a ____.
3. A number of judges who are engaged in a case are called a _____.
4. A collection of tools is called a ____.
5. A collection of poems is called ____.
6. A collection of different types of books is called_____.
7. A number of grapes or nuts on a bunch is called ____.
8. A collection of ducks, chickens or fowl is called a ____.
9. A number of directors of any institution are called a _____.
10. A number of lions are called a ____.
11. A number of stars in the sky is called a _____.

12. A group of bacteria is called a ___.

13. A group of penguins is called a ___.

14. A group of fish is called a ____.

15. A number of cards are called a _____.

Exercise 4. Complete the following sentences using appropriate collective nouns.

1. A .... of locusts attacked a .... of cattle.

2. A .... of birds is always a beautiful sight.

3. They welcomed the chief guest with a .... of flowers.

4. As we drove down the country side, we saw a .... of sheep grazing in the fields.

5. The ....of thieves has been arrested by the police.

6. There we saw a man carrying a .... of clothes on his head.

7. A .... of musicians was hired to perform at the party.

8. My friend has a fine .... of old stamps.

CHAPTER THREE

Adjective

An **adjective** describes or modifies <u>noun</u>/s and <u>pronoun</u>/s in a sentence. It normally indicates quality, size, shape, duration, feelings, contents, and more about a noun or pronoun.

Adjectives usually provide relevant information about the nouns/pronouns they modify/describe by answering the questions: *What kind? How many? Which one? How much?* Adjectives enrich your writing by adding precision and originality to it.

Example:

- The team has a dangerous batsman. (What kind?)
- I have ten candies in my pocket. (How many?)
- I loved that red car. (Which one?)
- I earn more money than he does. (How much?)

However, there are also many adjectives which do not fit into these questions. Adjectives are the most used parts of speech in sentences. There are several types of adjectives according to their uses.

Types of Adjectives

- <u>Descriptive Adjectives</u>
- <u>Quantitative Adjectives</u>
- <u>Proper Adjectives</u>

- <u>Demonstrative Adjectives</u>
- <u>Possessive Adjectives</u>
- <u>Interrogative Adjectives</u>
- <u>Indefinite Adjectives</u>
- <u>Articles</u>
- <u>Compound Adjectives</u>

Descriptive Adjectives:

A **descriptive adjective** is a word which describes nouns and pronouns. Most of the adjectives belong in this type. These adjectives provide information and attribute to the nouns/pronouns they modify or describe. Descriptive adjectives are also called **qualitative adjectives.**

Participles are also included in this type of adjective when they modify a noun.

Examples:

- I have a fast car. (The word 'fast' is describing an attribute of the car)
- I am hungry. (The word 'hungry' is providing information about the subject)
- The hungry cats are crying.
- I saw a flying Eagle.

Quantitative Adjectives:

A **quantitative adjective** provides information about the quantity of the nouns/pronouns. This type belongs to the question category of 'how much' and 'how many'.

Examples:

- I have 20 bucks in my wallet. (How much)
- They have three children. (How many)
- You should have completed the whole task. (How much)

Proper Adjectives:

Proper adjectives are the adjective form of <u>proper nouns</u>. When proper nouns modify or describe other nouns/pronouns, they become proper adjectives. 'Proper' means 'specific' rather than 'formal' or 'polite.'

A proper adjective allows us to summarize a concept in just one word. Instead of writing/saying 'a food cooked in Chinese recipe' you can write/say 'Chinese food'.

Proper adjectives are usually capitalized as proper nouns are.

Example:

- American cars are very strong.
- Chinese people are hard workers.
- I love KFC burgers.
- Marxist philosophers despise capitalism.

Demonstrative Adjectives:

A **demonstrative adjective** directly refers to something or someone. Demonstrative adjectives include the words: *this, that, these, those.*

A <u>demonstrative pronoun</u> works alone and does not precede a noun, but a demonstrative adjective always comes before the word it modifies.

Examples:

- That building is so gorgeously decorated. ('That' refers to a singular noun far from the speaker)

- This car is mine. ('This' refers to a singular noun close to the speaker)
- These cats are cute. ('These' refers to a plural noun close to the speaker)
- Those flowers are heavenly. ('Those' refers to a plural noun far from the speaker)

Possessive Adjectives:

A **possessive adjective** indicates possession or ownership. It suggests the belongingness of something to someone/something.

Some of the most used possessive adjectives are *my, his, her, our, their, your.*

All these adjectives always come before a noun. Unlike <u>possessive pronouns</u>, these words demand a noun after them.

Examples:

- My car is parked outside.
- His cat is very cute.
- Our job is almost done.
- Her books are interesting.

Interrogative Adjectives:

An **interrogative adjective** asks a question. An interrogative adjective must be followed by a noun or a pronoun. The interrogative adjectives are: *which, what, whose.* These words will not be considered as adjectives if a noun does not follow right after them. '*Whose*' also belongs to the possessive adjective type.

Examples:

- Which phone do you use?
- What game do you want to play?
- Whose car is this?

Indefinite Adjectives:

An **indefinite adjective** describes or modifies a noun unspecifically. They provide indefinite/unspecific information about the noun. The common indefinite adjectives are *few, many, much, most, all, any, each, every, either, nobody, several, some,* etc.

Examples:

- I gave some candy to her.
- I want a few moments alone.
- Several writers wrote about the recent incidents.
- Each student will have to submit homework tomorrow.

When compound nouns/combined words modify other nouns, they become a compound adjective. This type of adjective usually combines more than one word into a single lexical unit and modifies a noun. They are often separated by a hyphen or joined together by a quotation mark.

Example:

- I have a broken-down sofa.
- I saw a six-foot-long snake.
- He gave me an "I'm gonna kill you now" look.

The Degree of Adjectives:

There are three degrees of adjectives: *Positive, comparative, superlative.*

These degrees are applicable only for the descriptive adjectives.

Examples:

Positive degree: He is a good boy.

Comparative degree: He is better than any other boy.

Superlative: He is the best boy.

Some important degree of adjective are as follows:

Positive

Comparative

Superlative

Angry
Angrier
Angriest
Bad
Worse
Worst
Big
Bigger
Biggest
Beautiful
More beautiful
Most Beautiful
Black
Blacker
Blackest
Clean
Cleaner
Cleanest
Clever
Cleverer
Cleverest
Cold
Colder
Coldest
Cool
Cooler
Coolest
Cruel
More Cruel
Most Cruel
Dear
Dearer
Dearest
Deep
Deeper

Deepest
Difficult
More Difficult
Most Difficult
Easy
Easier
Easiest
Empty
Emptier
Emptiest
Famous
More Famous
Most Famous
Fast
Faster
Fastest
Fat
Fatter
Fattest
Fine
Finer
Finest
Foolish
More Foolish
Most Foolish
Full
Fuller
Fullest
Funny
Funnier
Funniest
Good
Better
Best
Great

Greater
Greatest
Green
Greener
Greenest
Happy
Happier
Happiest
Hard
Harder
Hardest
Heavy
Heavier
Heaviest
High
Higher
Highest
Hot
Hotter
Hottest
Hungry
Hungrier
Hungriest
Late
Later
Latest
Large
Larger
Largest

Degrees of Adjectives list 2

Steep
Steeper
Steepest

Spicy
Spicier
Spiciest
Sour
Sourer
Sourest
Sorry
Sorrier
Sorriest
Sore
Sorer
Sorest
Soon
Sooner
Soonest
Soft
Softer
Softest
Smooth
Smoother
Smoothest
Smoky
Smokier
Smokiest
Smelly
Smellier
Smelliest
Smart
Smarter
Smartest
Small
Smaller
Smallest
Slow
Slower

Slowest
Slim
Slimmer
Slimmest
Sleepy
Sleepier
Sleepiest
Skinny
Skinnier
Skinniest
Sincere
Sincerer
Sincerest
Simple
Simpler
Simplest
Silly
Sillier
Silliest
Shy
Shyer
Shyest
Short
Shorter
Shortest
Shiny
Shinier
Shiniest
Sharp
Sharper
Sharpest
Shallow
Shallower
Shallowest
Scary

Scarier
Scariest
Sane
Saner
Sanest
Salty
Saltier
Saltiest
Safe
Safer
Safest
Sad
Sadder
Saddest
Rusty
Rustier
Rustiest
Rude
Ruder
Rudest
Rough
Rougher
Roughest
Roomy
Roomier
Roomiest
Risky
Riskier
Riskiest
Ripe
Riper
Ripest
Rich
Richer
Richest

Renowned
More renowned
Most renowned
Raw
Rawer
Rawest
Rare
Rarer
Rarest
Quiet
Quieter
Quietest
Quick
Quicker
Quickest
Pure
Purer
Purest
Proud
Prouder
Proudest
Pretty
Prettier
Prettiest
Popular
More popular
Most popular
Poor
Poorer
Poorest
Polite
Politer
Politest
Steep
Steeper

Steepest
Spicy
Spicier
Spiciest
Sour
Sourer
Sourest
Sorry
Sorrier
Sorriest
Sore
Sorer
Sorest
Soon
Sooner
Soonest
Soft
Softer
Softest
Smooth
Smoother
Smoothest
Smoky
Smokier
Smokiest
Smelly
Smellier
Smelliest
Smart
Smarter
Smartest
Small
Smaller
Smallest
Slow

Slower
Slowest
Slim
Slimmer
Slimmest
Sleepy
Sleepier
Sleepiest
Skinny
Skinnier
Skinniest
Sincere
Sincerer
Sincerest
Simple
Simpler
Simplest
Silly
Sillier
Silliest
Shy
Shyer
Shyest
Short
Shorter
Shortest
Shiny
Shinier
Shiniest
Sharp
Sharper
Sharpest
Shallow
Shallower
Shallowest

Scary

Scarier

Scariest

Sane

Saner

Sanest

Salty

Saltier

Saltiest

Safe

Safer

Safest

Sad

Sadder

Saddest

Rusty

Rustier

Rustiest

Rude

Ruder

Rudest

Rough

Rougher

Roughest

Roomy

Roomier

Roomiest

Risky

Riskier

Riskiest

Ripe

Riper

Ripest

Rich

Richer

Richest
Renowned
More renowned
Most renowned
Popular
More popular
Most popular
Poor
Poorer
Poorest
Polite
Politer
Politest
Plain
Plainer
Plainest
Old
Older/elder
Oldest/eldest
Oily
Oilier
Oiliest
Odd
Odder
Oddest
Noisy
Noisier
Noisiest
Nice
Nicer
Nicest
New
Newer
Newest

Degrees of adjectives list 3

Needy
Needier
Neediest
Neat
Neater
Neatest
Near
Nearer
Nearest
Naughty
Naughtier
Naughtiest
Nasty
Nastier
Nastiest
Narrow
Narrower
Narrowest
Moist
Moister
Moistest
Mild
Milder
Mildest
Messy
Messier
Messiest
Mean
Meaner
Meanest
Many
More
Most

Mad
Madder
Maddest
Low
Lower
Lowest
Lovely
Lovelier
Loveliest
Loud
Louder
Loudest
Long
Longer
Longest
Lonely
Lonlier
Loneliest
Lively
Livelier
Liveliest
Little (size)
Littler
Littlest
Little (amount)
Less
Least
Likely
Likelier
Likeliest
Light
Lighter
Lightest
Lazy
Lazier

Laziest
Late
Later
Latest
Large
Larger
Largest
Kind
Kinder
Kindest
Juicy
Juicier
Juiciest
Itchy
Itchier
Itchiest
Icy
Icier
Iciest
Young
Younger
Youngest
Worthy
Worthier
Worthiest
Worldly
Worldlier
Worldliest
Wise
Wiser
Wisest
Windy
Windier
Windiest
Wild

Wilder
Wildest
Wide
Wider
Widest
Wet
Wetter
Wettest
Weird
Weirder
Weirdest
Wealthy
Wealthier
Wealthiest
Weak
Weaker
Weakest
Warm
Warmer
Warmest
Ugly
Uglier
Ugliest
TRUE
Truer
Truest
Tough
Tougher
Toughest
Tiny
Tinier
Tiniest
Thirsty
Thirstier
Thirstiest

Thin
Thinner
Thinnest
Thick
Thicker
Thickest
Tasty
Tastier
Tastiest
Tan
Tanner
Tannest
Tall
Taller
Tallest
Sweet
Sweeter
Sweetest
Sweaty
Sweatier
Sweatiest
Sunny
Sunnier
Sunniest
Strong
Stronger
Strongest
Strict
Stricter
Strictest
Strange
Stranger
Strangest
Stingy
Stingier

Stingiest
Popular
More popular
Most popular
Poor
Poorer
Poorest
Polite
Politer
Politest
Plain
Plainer
Plainest
Old
Older/elder
Oldest/eldest
Oily
Oilier
Oiliest
Odd
Odder
Oddest
Noisy
Noisier
Noisiest
Nice
Nicer
Nicest
Young
Younger
Youngest
Worthy
Worthier
Worthiest
Worldly

Worldlier
Worldliest
Wise
Wiser
Wisest
Windy
Windier
Windiest
Wild
Wilder
Wildest
Wide
Wider
Widest
Wet
Wetter
Wettest
Weird
Weirder
Weirdest
Wealthy
Wealthier
Wealthiest
Weak
Weaker
Weakest
Warm
Warmer
Warmest
Ugly
Uglier
Ugliest
TRUE
Truer
Truest

Tough
Tougher
Toughest
Tiny
Tinier
Tiniest
Thirsty
Thirstier
Thirstiest
Thin
Thinner
Thinnest
Thick
Thicker
Thickest
Tasty
Tastier
Tastiest
Tan
Tanner
Tannest
Tall
Taller
Tallest
Sweet
Sweeter
Sweetest
Sweaty
Sweatier
Sweatiest
Sunny
Sunnier
Sunniest
Strong
Stronger

Strongest
Strict
Stricter
Strictest

Important degree of adjectives list 4

Strange
    Stranger
    Strangest
    Stingy
    Stingier
    Stingiest
    Steep
    Steeper
    Steepest
    Spicy
    Spicier
    Spiciest
    Sour
    Sourer
    Sourest
    Sorry
    Sorrier
    Sorriest
    Sore
    Sorer
    Sorest
    Soon
    Sooner
    Soonest
    Soft
    Softer
    Softest
    Smooth

Smoother
Smoothest
Smoky
Smokier
Smokiest
Smelly
Smellier
Smelliest
Smart
Smarter
Smartest
Small
Smaller
Smallest
Slow
Slower
Slowest
Slim
Slimmer
Slimmest
Sleepy
Sleepier
Sleepiest
Skinny
Skinnier
Skinniest
Sincere
Sincerer
Sincerest
Simple
Simpler
Simplest
Silly
Sillier
Silliest

Shy
Shyer
Shyest
Short
Shorter
Shortest
Shiny
Shinier
Shiniest
Sharp
Sharper
Sharpest
Shallow
Shallower
Shallowest
Scary
Scarier
Scariest
Sane
Saner
Sanest
Salty
Saltier
Saltiest
Safe
Safer
Safest
Sad
Sadder
Saddest
Rusty
Rustier
Rustiest
Rude
Ruder

Rudest
Rough
Rougher
Roughest
Roomy
Roomier
Roomiest
Risky
Riskier
Riskiest
Ripe
Riper
Ripest
Rich
Richer
Richest
Renowned
More renowned
Most renowned
Raw
Rawer
Rawest
Rare
Rarer
Rarest
Quiet
Quieter
Quietest
Quick
Quicker
Quickest
Pure
Purer
Purest
Proud

Prouder
Proudest
Pretty
Prettier
Prettiest
Young
Younger
Youngest
Worthy
Worthier
Worthiest
Worldly
Worldlier
Worldliest
Wise
Wiser
Wisest
Windy
Windier
Windiest
Wild
Wilder
Wildest
Wide
Wider
Widest
Wet
Wetter
Wettest
Weird
Weirder
Weirdest
Wealthy
Wealthier
Wealthiest

Weak
Weaker
Weakest
Warm
Warmer
Warmest
Ugly
Uglier
Ugliest
TRUE
Truer
Truest
Tough
Tougher
Toughest
Tiny
Tinier
Tiniest
Thirsty
Thirstier
Thirstiest
Thin
Thinner
Thinnest
Thick
Thicker
Thickest
Tasty
Tastier
Tastiest
Tan
Tanner
Tannest
Tall
Taller

Tallest
Sweet
Sweeter
Sweetest
Sweaty
Sweatier
Sweatiest
Sunny
Sunnier
Sunniest
Strong
Stronger
Strongest
Strict
Stricter
Strictest
Strange
Stranger
Strangest
Stingy
Stingier
Stingiest
Steep
Steeper
Steepest
Spicy
Spicier
Spiciest
Sour
Sourer
Sourest
Sorry
Sorrier
Sorriest
Sore

Sorer

Sorest

Soon

Sooner

Soonest

Soft

Softer

Softest

Smooth

Smoother

Smoothest

Exercise 1. Decide whether you have to use much or many:

1. We saw ______ animals at the zoo.
2. How ______ oranges did you put in the box?
3. There isn't ______ sugar in my coffee.
4. I don't have _______ friends.
5. The old man hasn't got ______ hair on his head.
6. I've packed ______ bottles of water.
7. I didn't get ______ sleep last night.
8. How ______ fruit do you eat in an average day?

Exercise 2. Decide whether you have to use a little or a few:

1. Can you please buy ________ apples.
2. We need ________ water.
3. I have ________ money left.
4. I take ________ sugar with my coffee.
5. We had ________ pints of beer there.
6. You have ________ time left.
7. There are ________ chairs in the room.
8. He only spent ________ dollars there.

Exercise 3. Decide whether you have to use some or any:

1. Is there _________ milk left?
2. There is _________ juice in the bottle.
3. Do you have _________ coffee?
4. I don't have _________ money left.
5. She has _________ money.
6. Do you know _________ of these singers?
7. I don't know _________ of them.
8. I know _________ of them.

Exercise 4. Decide whether you have to use some or many:

1. The child put _________ sand into the bucket.
2. I can lend you _________ money if you need it.
3. There aren't _________ pears left. Only two.
4. We had _________ cake with the tea.
5. Don't eat so _________ sweets or you'll get fat.
6. I had _________ beer last night at the bar.
7. I don't have _________ friends.
8. He brought _________ food with him.

Exercise 5. Decide whether you have to use little or less:

1. I have _________ interest in classical music.
2. I have _________ faith in him.
3. We need _________ furniture in this dance hall than in the big one.
4. You have to drink _________ coffee.
5. He has _________ money than I thought.
6. Tonight I drank _________ wine than last night.
7. She dedicates _________ time to her homework than to her hobbies.
8. This will take _________ time to finish than the last time we tried.

Exercise 6. Decide whether you have to use a little or a lot:

1. That may cost you _________ of money.
2. I added ________ sugar to the mix.
3. You'll have to spend ________ of cash on this car. (a lot)
4. I can do it with ________ help from my friends.
5. ________ change can really make a difference.
6. I don't have ________ of free time today.
7. He left ________ of laundry for me to do.
8. She gave him ________ attention.

Exercise 7. Decide whether you have to use few or little:

1. There's ________ point in calling.
2. ________ people understood what he said.
3. There is ________ use in trying to do this.
4. There's ________ space here as it is.
5. There's ________ I can do about this.
6. Dan is a great student. He has ________ problems with history.
7. There was ________ traffic on the road.
8. I think Coventry will win the match but ________ people agree with me.

Exercise 8. Decide whether you have to use farther or further:

1. How much ________ do you plan to drive tonight?
2. I just can't go any ________.
3. Do you have any ________ plans for adding on to the building?
4. That's a lot ________ than I want to carry this heavy suitcase!
5. The ________ that I travel down this road, the ________ behind schedule I get.
6. How much ________ do you intend to take this legal matter?
7. It's not that much ________ to the gas station.
8. How much ________ do I have to run, coach?

Exercise 9. Decide whether you have to use later or latter:

1. My neighbors have a son and a daughter: the former is a teacher, andthe _________ is a nurse.
2. I will address that at a _________ time.
3. Of the first two Harry Potter books, I prefer the _________.
4. John arrived at the party _________ than Mary did.
5. I prefer the _________ offer to the former one.
6. I will be back _________.
7. I was given the choice between a hamburger or a hotdog, I chose the _________ of the two; the hotdog.
8. When it comes to soy burgers or a juicy cow burger, I prefer the _________.

Exercise 10. Use the superlative form of the adjectives in brackets.

1. Who is the.............(tall) person in your family?
2. My mum is the................(good) cook in the world.
3. December is the.............(cold) month of the year in my country.
4. What's the..................(dangerous) animal in the world?
5. Ethan is the................ (happy) boy that I know.
6. Where are the..................(nice) beaches in your country?
7. She bought the................(big) cake in the shop.
8. Who is the.....................(famous) singer in your country?

CHAPTER FOUR

Articles

An article is a kind of determiner which is always used with and gives some information about a noun. They specify the definiteness of the noun. There are three articles used in English language- 'a', 'an', 'the'. Every noun must be accompanied by the article, if any, corresponding to its definiteness, and the lack of an article itself specifies a certain definiteness. Given the frequency with which they appear, these words are certainly indispensable to the language.

Therefore, this module will discuss articles for the benefit of the MBA aspirants to help them improve their language skills and become aware of one of the components of English grammar

Articles are divided into two categories:

Indefinite Article

Indefinite articles are used:
- with countable nouns when we don't know exactly which one we are referring to.

For instance,

- The teacher is talking about a ten year old boy
- I saw <u>a movie</u> last night
- I ate <u>an apple</u> pie today
- It costs <u>a hundred</u> rupees
- I eat <u>an orange</u> every day for breakfast

- while referring to a particular member of a group.
For instance,

- John is a Catholic
- Be <u>a responsible</u> citizen of the country
- Raghav is <u>an amazing</u> dancer

- to say what someone is or what job they do.
For instance,

- He is a teacher.
- Jane is <u>a chef</u>
- My son is <u>an ornithologist</u>

- with a singular noun to refer to all things of that kind.
For instance,

- A dog is man's best friend
- <u>An applea day</u>, keeps doctor away
- It was <u>an urgent</u> requirement

There are two types of indefinite articles:
-'a' is used with words starting with consonant sounds, for example, a doctor, a boy, a car, a university, a week, a house etc.
-'an' is used with words starting with vowel sounds, for example, an engineer, an orange, an honest man an elephant, an angle, an ice-cream, an octopus, an MBA exam etc.

Definite Article

There is only one definite article, 'the'. Definite article is used before a noun when we believe the listener knows exactly what we referring to
- because there is only one.
For instance,

- The President of India is going to visit the US soon
- <u>The apple pie</u> I tasted yesterday was delicious
- <u>the movie</u> I saw last night was boring
- the fajitas were spicy
- Amitabh Bachchan is <u>the one</u> and only mega star

- because we have already mentioned it.
For instance,

- A terrorist entered the mall. The terrorist was accompanied by three other men
- We bought <u>a dozen apples</u> today. They are <u>the yummiest apples</u>
- Mom baked <u>a cake</u> last night. <u>The cake</u> was delicious

We also use definite article with:
- countries whose names include words like kingdom, states or republic-the United Kingdom, the Kingdom of Nepal and <u>The</u> Republic of Congo or <u>The</u> United States of America.
- mountain ranges, group of islands, rivers, seas, oceans and canals-the Himalayas, the Atlantic, the Arabian Sea, The Gibraltar, The Andamans, The Rocky Mountains, The Bahamas
- newspapers-The Times of India, The Washington Post, The Hindu
- organisations: the United Nations, The IIMs, The University of Oxford
- with superlatives: the brightest student, the longest river, the most significant achievement

Question: Complete the following sentences by filling in 'a' or 'an' or 'the' as may be suitable

1. I am a fan of __ Greek culture.
2. I dread ____ principle is furious.
3. Dan was __ assistant director in that movie.
4. We live in ___ united community.
5. He loves playing ___ hornet.
6. Is there __ 'm' in your name.

7. Where are __ apricots your uncle sent.
8. My birthday is on __ 6th of May.
9. ___ Netherlands is still under ___ lockdown.
10. I have ___ important information for you.
11. Abhijit Banerjee is __ Nobel prize winner.
12. ___ Mehta's invited their friends and family.
13. Onions cost __ whooping $10 __ pound.
14. Where is ___ busiest city in ___ world.
15. My dog is ___ Dalmatian.
16. ___ migrant workers need our help.
17. Jane heard __ siren and panicked.
18. I still remember ___ summer of '69.
19. I am on __ UN mission.
20. Abhijit Banerjee won __ Nobel prize in Economics.
21. Rob wants __ hour off.
22. He is ___ European boy.
23. Mumbai is ___ busy city.
24. MBA Rendezvous is ___ excellent web portal to get __ latest MBA related news.

The definite article: 'the': At a glance

The definite article *the* is the most frequent word in English.

We use the definite article in front of a **noun** when we believe the **listener/reader knows** exactly what we are referring to:

- because there is **only one:**

   The Pope *is visiting Russia.*
   The moon *is very bright tonight.*
   Who is **the president of France?**

   This is why we use the definite article **with a superlative adjective:**

*He is **the tallest boy** in the class.*
*It is **the oldest building** in the town.*

- because there is **only one in that context:**

*We live in a small house next to **the church**.* (= the church in our village)
*Dad, can I borrow **the car**?* (= the car that belongs to our family)
*When we stayed at my grandmother's house, we went to **the beach** every day.* (= the beach near my grandmother's house)
*Look at **the boy** over there.* (= the boy I am pointing at)

- because we have **already mentioned** it:

*A young man got a nasty shock when he tried to rob a jewellery shop in Richmond. **The man** used a heavy hammer to smash the windows in **the shop**.*

We also use the definite article:

- to say something about **all the things** referred to by a noun:

***The wolf** is not really a dangerous animal.* (= Wolves are not really dangerous animals.)
***The kangaroo** is found only in Australia.* (= Kangaroos are found only in Australia.)
***The heart** pumps blood around the body.* (= Hearts pump blood around bodies.)

We use the definite article in this way to talk about **musical instruments:**

*Joe plays **the piano** really well.*
*She is learning **the guitar**.*

- to refer to a **system** or **service:**

*How long does it take on **the train?***
*I heard it on **the radio.***
*You should tell **the police.***

We can also use the definite article with <u>adjectives</u> like *rich*, *poor*, *elderly* and *unemployed* to talk about groups of people:

*Life can be very hard for **the poor.***
*I think **the rich** should pay more taxes.*
*She works for a group to help **the disabled**.*

Uses of the article the

The definite article 'the' is used in the following cases.

1. When a singular noun represents a whole class.

The camel is a beast of burden. (Here the singular noun camel is used to refer to all the camels.)

Note that when a plural noun is used to talk about things in general, articles are usually omitted.

Camels are beasts of burden.
Computers are expensive.

More examples are given below:

The whale is a kind of mammal.
The rose smells sweet.

Note that the article 'the' is never used before the nouns 'man' and 'woman' when they represent the whole class.

Man is mortal. (NOT The man is mortal.)

2. While speaking of something or somebody already referred to

The boy who came to see me yesterday was my brother.
The story that he told us yesterday was very interesting.

3. While speaking of a particular person or thing

The poor beggar could get no alms.

4. When you refer to classics and holy books

Examples are: The Ramayana; The Mahabharata; The Iliad

Note that when the author's name is mentioned with the book, the article is usually omitted.

Homer's Iliad (NOT Homer's the Iliad)

5. While referring to the names of journals and newspapers

The New York Times

The Wall Street Journal

6. When we refer to imaginary geographical lines

Examples are: The equator; the Tropic of Cancer; the Tropic of Capricorn; the latitude; the longitude

Exercise 1. Fill up the blanks with suitable articles:

1. .....old man wanted to see you in the morning.
2. John built... yard for his cattle.
3. She ate only....... orange for her breakfast.
4. My grandmother told me...... story.
5. Mr. Nautiyal bought........ new car.
6. My son is...... M.A from Agra University.
7. Rohan is .... intelligent son of....... poor farmer.
8. Neha lodged......... F.I.R. against the cheat.
9. Pass me......... slice of bread.
10. Rita has gone on......... month's vacation.
11. Narayanpur is......... small village.
12. Visitors can meet the patient only twice....... day.
13. There was....... elephant in the field.
14. Ravi made.......... error of judgement.
15. He was late by...... hour for the meeting.
16. Suresh has........ interest in acting.
17. Sita's brother is ....engineer in......... reputed company.
18. There is......... eucalyptus tree near my house.
19. She is..... honorary secretary of the club.
20. We met....... European girl in Rishikesh.

Exercise 2. Fill in the Blanks with appropriate articles:

1. ....village chief has started......... utensil shop.

2. Joya's father is.......... principal of our college.
3. ....Ganges flows from....... Himalayas.
4. Please give me...... copy of The Times of India.
5. Dhawans are particularly interested in music.
6. Market will remain closed for two days.
7. She wrote ...... paper for....... seminar.
8. Rohan bought........ cup of coffee.
9. ....earth moves round........ sun.
10. He met with....... accident yesterday.
11. Meeta saw........cat in....... garden.
12. We saw .....tiger in..... zoo.
13. Sunil's father is ......advocate in...... highcourt.
14. Suresh is........tallest boy in...... class.
15. She gave me.... call in the evening.
16. Dr. Hamid is...... urdu teacher.
17. I met .....boy...... boy was very polite.
18. Reading is...... good habit.
19. He is ......captain in....... army.
20. Mr. Gokhale is....... honorary president of our society.

CHAPTER FIVE

Pronouns

What is a Pronoun?

A pronoun is defined as a word or phrase that is used as a substitution for a **noun** or noun phrase, which is known as the pronoun's antecedent. Pronouns are short words and can do everything that nouns can do and are one of the building blocks of a sentence. Common pronouns are *he, she, you, me, I, we, us, this, them, that.* A pronoun can act as a subject, direct object, indirect object, object of the **preposition**, and more and takes the place of any person, place, animal or thing. So coffee becomes it, Barbara becomes she, Jeremy becomes he, the team becomes they, and in a sentence, *Barbara drinks a cup of coffee every afternoon* could become *she drinks a cup of it every afternoon,* or even *she drinks it every afternoon,* where the *it* would substitute *the cup of coffee,* not just the *coffee.*

Without pronouns, we'd constantly have to repeat nouns, and that would make our speech and writing repetitive, not to mention cumbersome. Without pronouns, *Barbara drinks a cup of coffee every afternoon, she likes to have it before dinner* would be *Barbara drinks a cup of coffee every afternoon, Barbara likes to have the cup of coffee before dinner.* Using pronouns helps the flow of sentences and makes them more interesting

- He

- It
- You
- I
- They
- We
- Who
- Him
- Them
- Whoever
- Anyone
- Something
- Nobody

Pronoun examples in the following sentences are in bold for easy identification.

1. Billy, Caren, and I were playing poker with friends -> **We** were playing poker with friends.
2. Ellie loves watching movies. -> **She** loves watching movies, especially if **they** are comedies.
3. Will Daniel be going to the circus with Sarah? -> Will **he** be going **there** with **her?**

As mentioned, pronouns are usually used to replace nouns, however they can also stand in for certain <u>adverbs</u>, <u>adjectives</u>, and other pronouns. Almost anytime you refer to a person, animal, place or thing, you can use pronouns to add interest and make your speech or writing flow better.

In nearly all cases, a pronoun must follow an expression called an antecedent. This basically means that a pronoun can only really be understood in the context of prior information about the noun. For example, if we use the pronoun *she* in a sentence, we will only be able to understand it if we know who *she* is, thus an antecedent, perhaps giving the person's name, is usually supplied first. In the example above *Barbara drinks a cup of coffee every afternoon*, if we had never mentioned Barbara or what she drinks, it would be unclear if we said, *She drinks it every afternoon.* Your reader would be confused and wonder who *she* is and what does she drink, wine, water, lemonade?

Once Barbara has been mentioned, we would use the pronouns *she* and *her* later in the writing in order to stop repeating the proper noun *Barbara* and possessive proper noun *Barbara's.*

Barbara went to the restaurant for dinner with **her** (Barbara's) friends. **She** (Barbara) was very hungry, but **her** (Barbara's) friends would not stop chatting. Eventually, Barbara decided to take matters into **her** (Barbara's) own hands and **she** (Barbara) demanded that **they** (Barbara's friends) stop talking.

Imagine how that sentence would read if it kept repeating **Barbara** and **Barbara's**. Pronouns have acted to make the writing tighter and, arguably, much more elegant. This is just a basic example of the use of pronouns, they act in many ways to help make speech and writing more lucid and dynamic.

Types of Pronouns

Pronouns can be divided into numerous categories including:

- <u>Indefinite pronouns</u> – those referring to one or more unspecified objects, beings, or places, such as someone, anybody, nothing. Notice in the examples below that there is no set position for where an indefinite pronoun will appear in a sentence.

  Indefinite pronoun examples:
  1. Anyone
  2. Somebody
  3. Whichever
  4. Whoever
  5. Other
  6. Something
  7. Nobody

Indefinite pronoun examples in the following sentences are in bold for easy identification.

- Would **anyone** like a coffee?
- Take **whatever** you like. Jamie took one cookie and Ben took the **other**.
- **Whoever** owns this is in big trouble! I want **someone to move this now**.

Indefinite pronouns can also be used to create sentences that are almost abstract. Examples could include: *this, all, such and something*.

- **All** was not lost.
- **Such** is life.
- **Something** tells me **this** won't end well.

- <u>Personal pronouns</u> – those associated with a certain person, thing, or group; all except you have distinct forms that indicate singular or plural number. Personal pronouns are always specific and are often used to replace a proper noun (someone's name) or a collective group of people or things. Personal pronouns have two main groups, one referring to the subject of the sentence and one to the object.
  The first is used to replace the subject of the sentence: *I, you, he, she, it, we, you and they*. Notice that *you* is repeated as *you* can be singular, addressing one person, or plural, addressing a group of people.

Personal pronoun examples in the following sentences are in bold for easy identification.

- Jack and David are friends. **They** play basketball together.
- **I** have more money than **he**
- **We** will be late if **you** don't hurry up.

The second group of pronouns replaces the object of the sentence: *me, you, him, her, it, us, you, them*. Consider the sentence again:

We will be late if **you** don't hurry up.

In the above example, *we* is the subject of the sentence, but *you* is the object. Other examples of pronouns replacing the object:

- Peter sang the song to **me**.
- Missing the train will cause **us** to be late.

She packed **them** tightly in the suitcase.

- <u>Reflexive pronouns</u> – those preceded by the adverb, adjective, pronoun, or noun to which they refer, and ending in –*self* or –*selves*. Reflexive pronouns are used to refer back to the subject or clause of a sentence. The list of reflexive pronouns includes: *Myself, yourself, himself, herself, itself, ourselves, yourselves, themselves*.
  Reflexive pronoun examples in the following sentences are in bold for easy identification.

  - Count **yourselves**
  - Annie only had **herself** to blame.

Peter and Paul had baked **themselves** cakes.

- <u>Demonstrative pronouns</u> – those used to point to something specific within a sentence. There are only four demonstrative pronouns – *this, that, these, those* – but the usage can be a bit tricky at times. *This* and *that* are singular, whereas *these* and *those* are plural. As you may have noticed, there can be some crossover with indefinite pronouns when using *this* and *that*.
  Demonstrative pronoun examples in the following sentences are in bold for easy identification.

- I prefer **this.**
- **These** are beautiful, but **those** belong to Danny.
- Did you see **that?**

While it can be confusing, **this, that, these** and **those** can sometimes be used as demonstrative adjectives. The difference between the two is that a demonstrative pronoun replaces the noun and a demonstrative adjective qualifies the noun.

I prefer this *photo*. These flowers are *beautiful,* but those *vases* belong to Danny. Did you see that *rainbow*?

It should be clear that this, that, these and those in the example above are not pronouns because they are being used to qualify the noun, but not replace it. A good trick for remembering the difference is that a demonstrative pronoun would still make sense if the word *one* or *ones* followed it in the sentence.

I prefer **this** (one). **These** (ones) are beautiful. Did you see **that** (one)? **Those** (ones) belong to Danny.

- <u>Possessive pronouns</u> – those designating possession or ownership. Examples include: *mine, its, hers, his, yours, ours, theirs, whose.* Consider the example:

  - This cat is **mine.**

Mine is indicating possession, that the cat belongs to me. Incidentally, *this* in the sentence is not a pronoun but demonstrative adjective as it qualifies the noun *cat.* You will find that possessive pronouns often follow phrases that contain demonstrative adjectives.

Possessive pronoun examples in the following sentences are in bold for easy identification.

  - Are these bananas **yours?**
  - This money is **ours.**

Is the fault **theirs** or **yours?**

- <u>Relative pronouns</u> –those which refer to nouns mentioned previously, acting to introduce an adjective (relative) clause. They will usually appear after a noun to help clarify the sentence or give extra information. Examples include: *who, which, that, whom, whose.* Consider the following sentence:
  The man *who* stole the car went to jail. The relative pronoun *who* acts to refer back to the noun *man.* It acts to open a clause by identifying the man as not just any man, but the one who stole the car.Relative pronoun examples in the following sentences are in bold for easy identification.

  - The table, **which** sits in the hallway, is used for correspondence.
  - The car **that** crashed into the wall was blue.
  - This is the woman, **whose** key you found.

- <u>Interrogative pronouns</u> –Those which introduce a question. Examples include: *who, whom, whose, what, which.* We can usually identify an interrogative pronoun by the fact that they often appear at the beginning of a question.
  Interrogative pronoun examples in the following sentences are in bold for easy identification.

  - **Who** will come to the party?
  - **Which** do you prefer?
  - **What** do you need?
  - **Whose** clothes are on the floor?
  - **Whom** did you tell?

Whom and who are often confused, and even native speakers will use them incorrectly. *Who* will replace the subject of a sentence, whereas *whom* will replace the direct or indirect object. A good tip for deciding which to use is that you can replace who in the sentence with a personal pronoun and it will still make sense. *Who will come to the party? I will come to the party*. The same system would not work for *Whom did you tell? I did you tell*.

- <u>Reciprocal pronouns</u> –Those expressing mutual actions or relationship; i.e. one another.
  There are just two reciprocal pronouns in English: *one another* and *each other*. They are mainly used to stop unnecessary repetition in a sentence, but also to reinforce the idea that collective and reciprocal actions are happening to more than one person or thing.John and Mary gave *each other* gifts. Using *each other* allows us the sentence to be more efficient than: John gave Mary a gift and Mary gave a gift to John. The countries worked with *one another* on national security. In this example, *one another* works to suggest that the action of working is being reciprocated back and forth by more than one country.

  Reciprocal pronoun examples in the following sentences are in bold for easy identification.

  - The boxers punched **each other**

  The couple love **one another** deeply

- <u>Intensive pronouns</u> – those ending in *–self* or *–selves* and that serve to emphasize their antecedents. These are almost identical to reflexive pronouns, but rather than just referring back to the subject of the sentence they work to reinforce the action. In many cases, the sentence would still make sense without the intensive pronoun.
  Intensive pronoun examples in the following sentences are in bold for easy identification.

  - I will do it **myself**.
  - We made this pie **ourselves**.

- ○ A nation speaks for **itself** through elections.

Notice how the intensive pronoun is working to emphasize the statement. The sentence would still technically be correct without the intensive pronoun, but it adds some important context to its meaning.

Pronoun Rules

There are a few important rules for using pronouns. As you read through these rules and the examples in the next section, notice how the pronoun rules are followed. Soon you'll see that pronouns are easy to work with.

- Subject pronouns may be used to begin sentences. For example: We did a great job.
- Subject pronouns may also be used to rename the subject. For example: It was she who decided we should go to Hawaii.
- Indefinite pronouns don't have antecedents. They are capable of standing on their own. For example: No one likes the sound of fingernails on a chalkboard.
- Object pronouns are used as direct objects, indirect objects, and objects of prepositions. These include: you, me, him, her, us, them, and it. For example: David talked to her about the mistake.
- Possessive pronouns show ownership. They do not need apostrophes. For example: The cat washed *its*

Examples of Pronouns

In the following examples, the pronouns are italicized.

1. *We* are going on vacation.
2. Don't tell *me* that *you* can't go with *us.*

3. *Anybody* who says *it* won't be fun has no clue *what they* are talking about.
4. *These* are terribly steep stairs.
5. *We* ran into *each other* at the mall.
6. I'm not sure *which* is worse: rain or snow.
7. *It* is one of the nicest Italian restaurants in town.
8. Richard stared at *himself* in the mirror.
9. The laundry isn't going to do *itself*.
10. *Someone* spilled orange juice all over the countertop!

Exercise 1. Choose the best answer to complete each sentence:

1. This is ____________ speaking.

    A. John
    B. He
    C. He john
    D. Am

2. Greg is as smart as ____________ is.

    A. I
    B. me
    C. she
    D. we

3. The dog chewed on ____________ favorite toy.

    A. it's
    B. it is
    C. its'
    D. its

4. It could have been ____________ .

  A. Jerry
  B. anyone
  C. better
  D. more difficult

5. Terry is taller than ____________ am.

  A. I
  B. me
  C. she
  D. we

Exercise 2: Write the correct possessive pronoun on a separate sheet of paper.

  1. Did you finish _____ homework?
  2. Eduardo is looking for _____ backpack.
  3. The TV has a scratch on _____ screen.
  4. The neighbors put up ______ Christmas lights early this year.
  5. ______ family values honesty and kindness.
  6. Shauna and ______ boyfriend are going to the dance together.
  7. ______ mom always told me to believe in myself.
  8. Have you bought Harrison a gift for _____ birthday?
  9. The mama cat takes good care of _____ kittens.

Exercise 3: Write the independent possessive pronoun on a separate sheet of paper.

1. You can order whatever you want. The choice is ______.
2. All my friends like to cook. Cooking is a favorite activity of ______.
3. My brother and I bought a car together to share, so it is ______.

4. The candy belongs to Sarah. It is ______.I bought the food, so it's
______.

Exercise 4. Write the proper pronoun on a separate sheet of paper.

1. Is this (your, yours, you're) wallet?During (their, theirs, there's) reign, the king and queen were fair and just.
2. Want to share (my, mine) salad with me?
3. See if the neighbors can help us cut down (our, ours, we) tree.
4. Ask Carlos for (he, his, her) phone number.
5. Don't touch (my, mine) phone; it's (my, mine).
6. Cats are known for (their, theirs, there's) agility.
7. My painting does not compare to (your, yours, you're).
8. If (your, yours, you're) mom says yes, you can come to my party.
9. The baseball team displayed (their, theirs, they're) trophy in the locker room.
10. What did your sister say about (her, his, hers) job interview?
11. I don't want to share (we, our, ours) work with the other team because it's (we, our, ours).
12. You left (your, yours, you're) keys over here.
13. Some friends of (their, theirs, there's) are spending the weekend.
14. Is that blue jacket mine or (your, yours, you're)?

CHAPTER SIX

Verb

A **verb** is a <u>word</u> or a combination of words that indicates action or a state of being or condition. A verb is the part of a <u>sentence</u> that tells us what the subject performs. Verbs are the hearts of English sentences.

Examples:

- Jacob <u>walks</u> in the morning. (A usual action)
- Mike <u>is going</u> to school. (A condition of action)
- Albert <u>does not like</u> to walk. (A negative action)
- Anna <u>is</u> a good girl. (A state of being)

Verbs are related to a lot of other factors like the *subject, person, number, tense, mood, voice,* etc.

Basic Forms of Verbs

There are **six basic** forms of verbs. These forms are as follows:

- **Base form:** Children <u>play</u> in the field.
- **Infinitive:** Tell them not <u>to play</u>
- **Past tense:** They <u>played</u> football yesterday.
- **Past participle:** I have <u>eaten</u> a burger.
- **Present participle:** I saw them <u>playing</u> with him today.
- **Gerund:** <u>Swimming</u> is the best exercise.

Different Types of Verbs

- Main/Base Verb
- Regular/Weak Verb
- Irregular/Strong Verb
- Transitive Verb
- Intransitive Verb
- Weak Verb
- Strong Verb
- Finite Verbs
- Non-finite Verbs
- Action Verbs
- Linking Verb
- Auxiliary Verbs
- Modal Verbs
- Reflexive Verb
- Ergative Verb
- Phrasal Verb
- Lexical Verb
- Delexical Verb
- Stative/Being Verb
- Dynamic Verb
- Non-continuous Verb
- Participle
- Gerund
- Infinitive

Base Verb

The **base verb** is the form of a verb where it has no ending (-ing, -ed, -en) added to it. It is also called the Root Verb since it is the very root form of a verb.

<u>Examples:</u>

- I **go** to school every day.
- You **run** a mile every morning.
- **Do** your homework.

Regular Verb

The Verbs that follow the most usual conjugations are considered **Regular Verbs**. It is regular since it abides by most if not all of the regular grammar rules there are.
<u>Examples:</u>

- Rehan **plays** cricket.
- Tam **called** out my name.
- You really **walked** all the way back?

Irregular Verb

The Verbs that have irregularities in terms of following grammar rules are Irregular Verbs, in general.
<u>Examples:</u>

- **Do** the dishes.
- I hardly ever **drink** enough water in a day.
- She **drove** all the way back.

Transitive Verb

The Main Verb that takes a direct object sitting right after it would be a Transitive Verb. They usually construct the most straightforward of sentences.

<u>Examples:</u>

- She **went** to the fair.
- We do not **like** being called out loud in crowds.
- I **love** visiting my village home.

Intransitive Verb

The main Verb that does not take a direct object specified right afterward and rather there is an indirect one mentioned somewhere along the line is called an Intransitive Verb. These verbs often make the corresponding sentences incomplete.

<u>Example:</u>

- I **laughed**.
- John **ran**.
- A ghast of cold wind **blew**.

Weak Verb

Verbs that end with "-d" and "-t" in their Past Indefinite and Past Participle form are Weak Verbs. There is a tendency to associate Weak Verbs with Regular Verbs but not all Weak Verbs are Regular Verbs in the English language.

Strong Verb

Strong Verbs are those in which the vowels in the verb stem changes from "i" to "a" to "u" in the Present Indefinite to Past Indefinite to Past Participle form of Verbs.

Finite Verbs

Finite verbs are the actual verbs that are called the roots of sentences. It is a form of a verb that is performed by or refers to a subject and uses one of the twelve forms of tense and changes according to the number/person of the subject.

Example:

- Alex <u>went</u> to school. (Subject – Alex – performed the action in the past. This information is evident only by the verb 'went'.)
- Robert <u>plays</u> hockey.
- He <u>is playing</u> for Australia.
- He <u>is</u> one of the best players. (Here, the verb 'is' directly refers to the subject itself.)

Non-finite Verbs

Non-finite Verbs are not actual verbs. They do not work as verbs in the sentence rather they work as nouns, adjectives, adverbs, etc. Non-finite verbs do not change according to the number/person of the subject because these verbs, also called **verbals**, do not have any direct relation to the subject. Sometimes they become the subject themselves.

The forms of non-finite verbs are – infinitive, gerund, and participle (participles become finite verbs when they take auxiliary verbs.)

Example:

- Alex went abroad <u>to play</u> (Infinitives)
- <u>Playing</u> cricket is his only job. (Present participle)
- I have a <u>broken</u> bat. (Past participle)
- <u>Walking</u> is a good habit. (Gerund)

Action Verbs

Action verbs indicate what the subject of a sentence performs. Action verbs can make the listener/reader feel emotions, see scenes more vividly and accurately.

Action verbs can be *transitive* or *intransitive*.

Transitive verbs must have a direct object. A transitive verb demands something/someone to be acted upon.

Example:

- I <u>painted</u> the car. (The verb 'paint' demands an object to be painted)
- She <u>is reading</u> the newspaper. (The verb 'read' asks the question "what is she reading?" – the answer is the object)

Intransitive verbs do not act upon anything. They may be followed by an adjective, adverb, preposition, or another part of speech.

Example:

- She <u>smiled</u>. (The verb 'smile' cannot have any object since the action of 'smiling' does not fall upon anything/anyone)
- I <u>wake</u> up at 6 AM. (No object is needed for this verb)

Linking Verb

A <u>linking verb</u> adds details about the subject of a sentence. In its simplest form, it connects the subject and the complement — that is, the words that follow the linking verb. It creates a link between them instead of showing action.

Often, what is on each side of a linking verb is equivalent; the complement redefines or restates the subject.

Generally, linking verbs are called *'be' verbs* which are - *am, is, are, was, were*. However, there are some other verbs that can work as linking verbs. Those verbs are:

Act, feel, remain, appear, become, seem, smell, sound, grow, look, prove, stay, taste, turn.

Some verbs in this list can also be action verbs. To figure out if they are linking verbs, you should try replacing them with forms of the *be verbs*. If the changed sentence makes sense, that verb is a linking verb.

Example:

- She <u>appears</u> ready for the game. (She <u>is</u> ready for the game.)
- The food <u>seemed</u> delicious. (The food <u>was</u> delicious.)
- You <u>look</u> happy. (You <u>are</u> happy.)

Auxiliary Verbs

Auxiliary verbs are also called *helping verbs*. An **auxiliary verb** extends the main verb by helping to show time, tense, and possibility. The auxiliary verbs are – *be verbs, have,* and *do.*

They are used in the continuous (progressive) and perfect tenses.

Linking verbs work as main verbs in the sentence, but auxiliary verbs help main verbs.

Do is an auxiliary verb that is used to ask questions, to express negation, to provide emphasis, and more.

Example:

- Alex <u>is</u> going to school.
- Thcy <u>arc</u> walking in the park.
- I <u>have</u> seen a movie.
- <u>Do</u> you drink tea?
- <u>Don't</u> waste your time.
- Please, <u>do</u> submit your assignments.

Modal Verbs

A **modal verb** is a kind of auxiliary verb. It assists the main verb to indicate possibility, potentiality, ability, permission, expectation, and obligation.

The modal verbs are *can, could, must, may, might, ought to, shall, should, will, would.*

Example:

- I <u>may</u> want to talk to you again.
- They <u>must</u> play their best game to win.
- She <u>should</u> call him.
- I <u>will</u> go there.

Reflexive Verb

When the Subject and the Object are the same and the Verb reflects on the Subject, that is the Reflexive Verb. These Verbs are often used with Reflexive Pronouns like - myself, himself, herself, itself etc.

<u>Examples:</u>

- He has done it himself.
- I'll watch it myself.

Phrasal Verb

An idiomatic phrase consisting of a Verb and another element, most likely an <u>Adverb</u> or a <u>Preposition</u> is called a Phrasal Verb.

<u>Examples:</u>

- She **broke down** in tears.
- Don't **look down upon** the poor.

- I'll **see to** it.

Lexical Verb

Lexical Verb is the main or principal verb of a sentence which typically takes the major responsibility of a Verb that represents the action of the Noun or Pronoun.
  <u>Examples:</u>

- He **ran** to his father.
- I **laughed** out loud.
- Rina **tried** her best.

DE-Lexical Verb

Delexical Verbs lack importance when it comes to meaning since these Verbs hardly have meanings of their own when used individually. The meaning is taken out of the Verbs and put into the Noun. Take, have, make, give etc. are Delexical Verbs.
  <u>Examples:</u>

- He **took** a shower.
- I **had** a cold drink.
- She **made** some arrangements.

Stative Verb

The Verbs that describe the state of being are called Stative or Being Verbs.
  <u>Examples:</u>

- I **need** some boxes.

- You **belong** to the pomp and power.
- He **smells** danger.
- They **remember** what happened that day.

Dynamic Verb

The Verbs that entail continuous or progressive action of the Subject are called Dynamic or Fientive Verbs. They express the Subject's state of being on the move.
Examples:

- He's **running** fast.
- Keep **hitting** the ball hard.
- The dog goes for a **walk** every afternoon.

Non-continuous Verb

The Verbs that are usually never used in their continuous forms are called Non-continuous Verbs.

Intensive Verb

The Verbs that focus intensely on just the Subject are called Intensive Verbs. Intensive Verbs are also called Linking or Copular Verbs.
Examples:

- You **seem** happy.
- It **appears** to be just perfect.
- She **looks** stunning.
- He's **become** rather irritable.

Extensive Verb

All the Verbs that do not focus intensively on just the Subject (as the Intensive Verbs) of the sentence are Extensive Verbs.
Examples:

- He **loves** her.
- She **runs** too fast.
- Ron **sells** fish.

Participle

A participle is a Verb form where they retain some of the characteristics and functions of both Verbs and adopt those of the Adjectives.
Examples:
Present Participle (Verb + -ing)

- Have I become a laughing stock?
- Cycling is a well-rounded exercise.

Past Participle

- I have taken a hint.
- Have you given it enough thought?

Perfect Participle (Having + Past Participle)

- Having said that, I was quite worried.
- Having stepped out of my comfort zone, I saw a whole new world.

Gerund

The Verbs having -ing endings that function like Nouns in sentences are called Gerunds.

Examples:

- **Smoking** is injurious to health.
- **Walking** is good for health.
- I love **swimming**.

Infinitive

The 'to + Verb' forms where the Verbs are at their base or stem forms while they function as Nouns, Adjectives or Adverbs instead of Verbs.

Examples:

- I wanted **to help** you out.
- Are you trying **to go** there?
- I just love **to flaunt** my new Ferarri.

Exercise 1. Fill the blanks with the correct form of verb:

1. We _____________ (has paid/have paid) him the money.
2. I _________ (have bought/has bought) my sister a watch.
3. _________ (Show/Shows) me your hands.
4. You _________ (has made/have made) your shirt dirty.
5. We _________ (are waiting/is waiting) for Rohan.
6. These books _________ (belong/belongs) to me.
7. She _________ (want/wants) to go.
8. We _________ (will like/would like) to visit the museum.
9. He _________ (has finished/have finished) talking.
10. My brother _________ (enjoy/enjoys) playing cricket.
11. We _________ (find/found) the house deserted.

12. We __________ (hope/hoped) that you would succeed.
13. She __________ (has assured/have assured) me that she is ready to help.
14. Nobody __________ (know/knows) when he will arrive.
15. We __________ (must find out/find) where to put it.
16. I __________ (shall show/show) you how to operate it.
17. Jack __________ (cannot/could not) decide what he should do next.
18. I __________ (can't/could not) imagine why she has behaved like that.
19. Can you __________ (tell/told/tells) me where he lives?

Exercise 2. Fill in the blanks with the correct form of verbs:

1. When he --------- (come) here, we ----------- (sleep).

2. They ------------(go) for walk often.

3. We ----------(take) tea in the morning generally.

4. Two and two -----------(make) four.

5. Rudra --------- (cut) grass this time.

6. When I -----------(g0) there, I will help him.

7. As soon as he ----------(enter) the house, the light ---------(go) off.

8. The farmer ---------(purchase) the seeds before it ------------ (rain).

9. After he ---------(take) his breakfast, he went to school.

10. I read this book after I ---------(return) from the market.

11. I wish I ---------(take) this medicine.

12. It is high time we ------- (start) this work.

13. They ---------(prepare) for exams for two years.

14. I ----------(write) a novel for six months this time next month.

15. When he arrived, I ---------(sleep) since morning.

16. The children -----------(make) a noise for the last ten minutes.

17. The teacher -----------(teach) this time tomorrow.

18. She ----------(prepare) food by this time tomorrow.

19. He said that he -----------(not tell) a lie.

20. He behaves as if he ----------(be) a king.

21. If he -----------(work) hard, he would have passed.

22. If you ------------(invite) me, I would certainly come.

23. If she ------------(start) now, she will compete the task in time.

24. India -----------(get) freedom in 1947.

25. They ------------(kill) the snake yesterday.

26. Would that we -------------(be) all birds !

27. Would that I -----------(know) him!

28. --------- you ---------(focus) on your studies, you could have got admission.

29. He -----------(take) tea yet.

30. We ----------(do) already our task.

CHAPTER SEVEN

Adverbs

Adverb and its types

An adverb qualifies a verb, an adjective and another adverb.
There are examples of adverb:

1. The boy run slowly.
2. Adverb use with adjective:
3. Klay did a very difficult sum.

In this example the word very is used as a adverb and difficult is used as adjective.
Adverb use with another adverb:
He run very quickly.
Here one adverb is very and other adverb is quickly so adverb use with another adverb.

Kinds of adverb

1. Adverb of manner
2. Adverb of place
3. Adverb of time
4. Adverb of frequency
5. Adverb of certainty

6. Adverb of degree
7. Adverb of interrogative

There are seven kinds of adverbs.

Adverb of manner

The adverb which is used for describing the manner of doing a work is called adverb of manner.it answer the question "how".

Examples of the adverb of manner are given below:

Badly, rightly, painfully are the examples of the adverb of manners.

Uses of adverb of manner in sentences:

1. You're looming not well in these days.
2. She speaks loudly.
3. She was running fast.
4. Women were doing their work quietly.

Adverb of place

The adverb which is used for describing the place of work is called adverb of place.

It answer the question "where".

The simple mean of adverb of place is describes the place of work.

Examples of the adverb of place:

1. There
2. Under
3. Behind
4. Up are the examples of the adverb of place.

Use of adverb of place in sentences:

1. I am going back to home.
2. She took the child outside.
3. I have nowhere to go.

Adverb of time

The adverb which describes the time and direction of the time or something is called adverb of time.

Examples of adverb of time:

1. Never
2. After
3. Yesterday
4. Early

Use of adverb of time in sentences:

1. She goes to picnic daily.
2. Always speak the truth.
3. They often play match.

Adverb of frequency

The adverb which is used for describing the frequency is called adverb of adver of frequency.

It answers the question how often.

Examples:

1. Often
2. Sometimes
3. Ever
4. seldom are the examples of the adverb of frequency.

Uses of adverb of frequency in sentences

1. we seldom meet.
2. They hardly ever eat out.
3. He is often late for work.

Adverb of certainty

This adverb describes the undoubted fact:

Adverb of certainty are given below

Absolutely, certainty, obviously, surely are the examples of the adverb of certainty.

Use of adverb of certainty in sentences:

1. He surely won't forget.
2. He is certainly a smart man.
3. She is definitely getting late.
4. They will obviously be punished by teacher.

Adverb of degree

The adverb which is used for describing the limit or degree of work is called adverb of degree.

Examples:

1. Very
2. Most
3. Quite
4. Enough
5. Fully are the examples of the adverb of degree.

Use of adverb of degrees in sentences:

1. Maria rather liked alay's impish ways.
2. My work is almost finished.
3. She helped me fully.

Interrogative adverb

When= at what time?
How= in what ways?
Why= for what place?
Examples:

1. How was she sitting?
2. Where was the bike park?
3. When did you hear about it?

Rules of Adverb

Rule I

Adjective qualifies a noun and a pronoun whereas **adverb** modifies a verb, an adjective and an adverb. For example
(i) Her act was remarkable. ($\sqrt{}$)
(ii) She acted remarkably to achieve success. ($\sqrt{}$)
(iii) She ran quicker than I. (Say 'more quickly' for 'quicker')
(iv) She is a very skilful dancer. ($\sqrt{}$)
(v) She dances very skilfully. ($\sqrt{}$)

Rule II

Adverbs of time such as 'Always, often, already, just, never, ever, sometimes, frequently, generally, recently, usually, seldom, hardly, rarely, normally etc** are generally placed before the verb they modify. For example

(i) My brother comes often every Sunday. (Place 'often' before 'comes')

(ii) He goes usually to the movie every Friday. (Place 'usually' before 'goes')

(iii) He never talks ill of friends. (√)

(iv) He is always satisfied. (√)

Rule III

Adverbs of manners are placed only after the Intransitive verb. However, the adverb can be placed **either before or after the transitive verb.** For example

(i) He returned immediately. (√)

(ii) He briefly narrated the incident to me. (√)

(iii) He narrated to me the incident briefly. (√)

(iv) He soundly slept last night. (Place 'soundly' after 'slept')

Rule IV

If the sentence is introduced by an adverb, inverted form of the verb is used for the sake of emphasis. e.g.

(i) Seldom he visits his parents. (✗)

(ii) Seldom does he visit his parents. (√)

(iii) He seldom visits his parents.(√)

(iv) Not seldom does he visit his parents. (√)

(v) Never I'll see her again. (√)

(vi) Never will I see her again.

(vii) I'll never see her again. (√)

(viii) She no sooner reached the station **than** she met her friend. (√)

(ix) No sooner did she reach the station **than** she met her friend. (√)

(x) She had hardly reached the station **when** the train arrived. (√)

(xi) Hardly/scarcely had she reached the station **when** the train arrived. (√)

(xii) So quickly she ran that she overtook her rivals. (Use 'so quickly did she run').

Rule V : Use of Else and Other

'**Else**' should be followed by '**but**'.

'**Other**' and '**otherwise**' are followed by 'than' e.g.

(i) It is nothing else than sheer madness. (Use 'but' in place of 'than')

(ii) She had no other alternative but stay here. (Use 'than' in place of 'but')

(iii) She has no one else to look after her except me. (Use 'but' in place of 'except')

Rule VI

Both '**never**' and '**not**' are adverbs. The use of 'never' for 'not' is incorrect. e.g.,

(i) I never went to Ooty last year. (Use 'did not' go in place of 'never')

(ii) I never remember to have said so. (Use 'do not' in place of 'never')

(iii) I remember never to have said so. (√)

Or

I don't remember to have said so.

(iv) I never allow my son to go out in dark. (Correct/habitual action)

Rule VII

Note the use of phrases.

'**Seldom or never**', '**seldom, if ever**', '**little or nothing**', '**little, if anything**'.

The phrases 'seldom or ever' and 'little or anything' are wrong in use. e.g.

(i) We seldom or ever meet our relatives these days. (✗)

(ii) We seldom or never (seldom, if ever) meet our relatives these days. (√)

Rule VIII

Negative adverbs should not be used with the words negative in meaning. So two negative should be avoided.

'Seldom, nowhere, never, nothing, hardly, scarcely, neither, barely, rarely' are some of the adverbs expressing negative meaning. e.g.

(i) I rarely went to meet nobody across the road. (Use 'anybody' in place of 'nobody')

(ii) She hardly knows somebody in the town. (Say 'anybody' in place of 'somebody')

(iii) I hardly know somebody in the town. (Say 'anybody' in place of 'somebody')

(iv) He does nothing without never consulting me. (Use 'ever' for 'never')

(v) They do not seldom come here. (Remove 'do not')

(vi) This will not help him, nothing ever does. (Use 'ever' for 'never')

(vii) He does not write well and I do not write neither. (Say 'either')

Note : (I) Avoid the use of negative, with 'deny, forbid' and 'both'.

(i) She denied that she had not given him books. (Delete 'not')

(ii) (a) Both of us are not going there. (✗)

(b) Neither of us is going there. (√)

(II) Avoid the use of negative with Conjunctions – **until, unless, lest**

Rule IX

Given below are some of the examples of the words being treated as adverbs whereas they are adjectives or nouns. e.g.,

(A) Manly, masterly, slovenly, monthly, weekly, sickly, friendly, orderly, gentlemanly are adjectives and should not be confused with adverbs.

(B) Coward, miser, niggard are nouns.

'Cowardly, miserly, niggardly' are adjectives.

'In a cowardly, miserly, niggardly manner' are used as adverbs.

(C) Fast, straight, outright, direct, hard, hardly, late, light, high, safe, quiet etc are used both as an adjective and adverb.

(D) 'Loudly' and 'Aloud' are adverbs though different in meanings. 'Loud' is an adjective.

(E) Late, lately

Late is both an adjective & an adverb

Lately is an adverb. (Recently)

(F)Hard is both an adjective and adverb used in affirmative sense.

Hardly is an adverb used in negative meaning. e.g.

(i) A soldier is trained never to fight cowardly. (Use 'in a cowardly manner')

(ii) I have never come across a coward Indian soldier. (Use 'cowardly' in place of 'coward')

(iii) The darkness closed in even as she was returning home fastly. (Use 'fast' in place of 'fastly')

(iv) You must learn to behave manly in the face of danger. (Use 'manfully' in place of 'manly')

(v) He is earning five hundred rupees monthly. (Say 'a month')

(vi) She is doing this work good these days. (Say 'well' for 'good')

(vii) Rohit always comes lately to school. (Say 'late' for 'lately')

(viii) He is coward. (Use 'a' before 'coward')

(ix) The teacher asked the students to talk loudly. (Say 'aloud')

(x) We must try to preserve hardly won freedom. (Use 'hard' in place of 'hardly')

(xi) Please keep the things in the room orderly. (Use 'in order' or 'in orderly manner' in place of 'orderly')

(xii) She rejected my application outrightly. (Say 'outright')

(xiii) Outright rejection of my plan disappointed me. (√)

Rule X

The use of '**very, much, so, too, enough, rather**'.

(**A**) '**Very**' modifies present participle used as adjective, adverb and adjective in positive degree. '**Much**' is used with comparative degree and past participle. e.g.,

(i) It is a much interesting picture. (Use 'very' in place of 'much')

(ii) I was very exhausted in the evening. (Use 'much' in place of 'very')

(iii) She did this work very quickly. (√)

(iv) She is much wiser than her mother. (√)

(v) She is very tired after a day's work. (√)

Note : Student should note the use of '**very**' and '**much**' in superlative degree. e.g.,

(i) She is **the very best** teacher in our school. (Here 'very' mean 'really')

(ii) She is **much the best** teacher in our school. (Here 'much' means 'decidedly')

(iii) She is **by far the** best teacher in our college. ('by far' means 'to a large extent')

(**B**) '**So**' and '**too**' should not be used without 'that' (Adverb clause) and 'to' (Infinitive) respectively.

'**Very**' and '**much**' may be used in the place of so and too.

(i) My brother is so healthy. (Use 'very' in place of 'so')

(ii) She is very kind. (Here 'very' means 'to a great extent')

(iii) She is too poor to study further. (√)

(iv) She is so poor that she cannot study further. (√)

(v) She is too healthy. (Over healthy) say 'very' for too)

(vi) It is too bad. (√)

(C) '**Enough**' is both an adjective and adverb. As an **adverb,** it is always placed after the adjective it modifies.

As an **adjective it** is placed before a noun. e.g.

(i) She is enough wise to allow her son to go. (Place 'enough' after 'wise')

(ii) He has enough money to spend. (√)

(iii) She is too kind to help everybody. (Say 'kind enough' very kind in place of 'too')

(iv) She is too weak to pass. (√)

(D) The use of 'rather'

(a) 'Rather' is an adverb of degree like 'fairly, quite, pretty (to some degree)'. e.g.,

(i) She is rather intelligent.

(ii) He is walking rather slowly.

(b) 'Rather' can also be used before a noun.e.g.,

(i) It is rather a nuisance.

(ii) It is rather a good step. (or a rather good step)

Note : Article 'a', 'an' should be placed before a noun. If there is an adjective with a noun, articles 'a', 'an' may be placed either before or after 'rather'.

(c) 'Rather' is also in case of preference- 'would rather, had rather, rather than' are used to express preference.

Rule XI

Note the difference between too, as well, also.

(a) 'Too, as well, also' are used in the sense of 'besides', 'in addition to' in affirmative sentences. But 'also' cannot be used at end position.

(i) She found her bag and money too/as well.

(ii) She plays the piano and the harmonium as well/too.

(iii) She found her bag and money also. (say 'also money')

(b) So + auxiliary + subject is used in affirmative sentences in relation to two persons doing one action.

(i) She won the prize and so did her sister. (win)

(ii) His wife plays piano and so does he. (play)

(c) Neither + auxiliary + subject is used in negative sentences in relation to two persons doing one action.

(i) He does not write well and neither do I. (write)

(ii) She will not lend money and neither will he. (lend)

Rule XII

While answering a question the adverb 'yes' or 'no' should be used according to the affirmative and negative answer. e.g.

(i) Have you taken food?

(ii) Yes, I have not taken so far? (Use 'No' in place of 'Yes')

Rule XIII

(A) Adverb 'as' should be used to introduce predicative of the verbs **'regard, describe, define, treat, view, know'**.

(B) Adverb 'as' should be avoided to introduce predicative of the verbs **'name, elect, think, consider, call, appoint, make, choose'** e.g.,

(i) I regard him my brother. (Add 'as' after 'him')

(ii) Science has been defined the study of nature. (Add 'as' after 'defined')

(iii) She is considered as the best dancer in the town. (Drop 'as' after 'considered')

(iv) The teacher called him as stupid. (Drop 'as')

(v) The principal appointed him as peon. (Remove 'as')

(vi) He thinks her as a fool. (Remove 'as')

(vii) He was elected as the secretary of our club. (Remove 'as')

CHAPTER EIGHT

Prepositions

What is a Preposition?

Sentences will not make any sense if prepositions are not present. Basically they indicate the relationship between the noun and the other words in the sentence. They show the relationships of sequence, space, and logic between the object and the rest of the sentence. They help us understand the order, time, connections and position.

We use a preposition to relate a noun or a pronoun to some other word in the sentence.

For example, in the sentence, "The players on the field are tired."

The preposition "on" shows the relationship between 'players' and 'field'.

What Exactly are called Prepositions?

A preposition is a tiny, common word that indicates direction (to in "a letter to you"), location (at in "at the door"), or time (in "by noon"), or that introduces an item (or in "a basket of apples"). The object of a preposition is usually a noun (noon), a noun phrase (the door), or a pronoun (you).

Prepositions show how other words in a sentence are related. Many prepositions indicate the location of something or the time it occurred. Because most prepositions have many definitions, their meaning varies greatly depending on the context. It is not a grammatical error to end a sentence with a preposition. Prepositions describe the location or timing of something in relation to something else. It's useful to have these specific words to tell us where monsters are while they're approaching. Are they in front of us or behind us? Will they show there in three seconds or at 12 a.m.?

Prepositions are frequently used to indicate the location of one noun in relation to another (e.g., The coffee is on the table beside you). However, they can also be used to convey more abstract concepts like purpose or contrast (e.g., We went for a walk despite the rain)

Some examples of Prepositions-

At, by, for, from, in, of, on, to, and with are the most prevalent prepositions. About, above, across, after, against, along, among, around, because of, before, behind, below, beneath, beside, between, close to, down, during, except, inside, instead of, into, like, near, off, on top of, onto, out of, outside, over, past, since, through, toward, under, until, up, upon, within, without.

Prepositions Come in a Variety of Forms

Direction, time, location, and geographical linkages, as well as other abstract sorts of relationships, are all indicated by prepositions.

Directions: Our destination can be found to the left.
Time: Since this morning, we've been working.
Location: We went to the theater to see a movie.
Example: Tonight, we'll be cooking for ten people.
Space: The dog hid beneath the table.
Example: Dan shared a meal with his boss.

How do prepositions help us?

Prepositions are known as the "largest small words" in English because, despite their modest length, they are crucial to the meaning of the phrase. A misplaced preposition can make all the difference between a well-written phrase and a tangle of words. Prepositions, on the other hand, provide the glue between elements of a sentence, allowing you to present your scientific findings more precisely and professionally when employed correctly.

Prepositions connect nouns, pronouns, or phrases (known as the preposition's object) to other words in a sentence. They show how their item is related to another word or component of the sentence in terms of time, space, or logic.

Examples:

1. The airplane flew over our house.
2. She sat on the chair.
3. The cups are kept above the plates.
4. The book belongs to Muskan.
5. They were sitting by the pool.
6. The dog jumped off the counter.
7. There is some curd in the fridge.
8. The napkin is placed beside the plate.
9. His house is across the street.
10. My book is next to the laptop.
11. The gas station is by the medical store.
12. I always go to work by bus.
13. Is the tea too hot for you?
14. The cat is hiding underneath the chair.
15. They have a discussion about cricket.

Preposition - An Explanation of Examples

1. Seema went to the mal

"To" is a preposition which shows direction.

1. What is the time on your watch?

"By" is a preposition which shows manners.

1. They arrived at the airport.

"At" is a preposition which shows time.

1. The bag is under the table.

"Under" is a preposition which shows place.

Kinds of Preposition

1. **Single Prepositions**

Prepositions which contain only one word are known as Single Prepositions. For eg- on, at, in, to for, of, from, up, etc.

- He was in the hotel for the party.
- She bought a gift for her son.
- The postmen left the parcel at the door.

1. **Double Prepositions**

When there is more than one word of prepositions present, it is known as Double preposition. For eg- Upto, within, etc.

- **Compound Preposition:** Compound prepositions consist of two or more words.

   For Example:

- **Participle Preposition:** Participle preposition consists of words that end in "ing". These are verbs which act as a preposition.

For Example:

- She talked regarding the social structure.
- Considering the fact that it is cloudy, it might rain tonight.
- Everyone attended the royal wedding, including the celebrities.

Preposition on the Basis of Functionality

Various types of prepositions on the basis of the functionality are:

1. **Preposition of Time**

This kind of preposition indicates when it indicates the time factor in the sentence. Pointing out an action which happened, happens or will happen in the future.
   Example

- Mahatma Gandhi was born on 2nd of October.
- I will reach there after sunset.
- Hope we can reach there before sunrise.

1. **Preposition of Place**

These kinds of prepositions are used to indicate a place or position. The most interesting thing is that the prepositions used in this are also in, at, on, which were used for time prepositions as well. But, there is nothing very you can easily understand about how to place them.
   Examples:

- Book is on the table.
- The bag is in the cupboard.
- We like books at the bookstore.

There are other prepositions of place as well like, Outside, inside, under, over, near.

1. **Preposition of Movement**

This preposition indicates the direction in which someone or something is moving. The most common preposition used is to.
Examples:

- We are going to the railway station.
- David went to the beach every day for a morning walk.
- He jumped into the swimming pool.

Some other examples are- Across, through, into, over, down, up, past, around.

1. **Prepositions of Manner**

These prepositions describe the way anything happens or any means by which it happens. Few such prepositions are by, like, in with and on.
Examples:

- Children go to school by bus.
- We went to a movie in a taxi.
- He played football like champions.

1. **Prepositions of Measure**

These kinds of prepositions show the quantity of something with someone or something.
Two main prepositions are by and of.
Examples:

- The Shopkeeper sells the cloth by metres.

- Richard bought four kilos of tomatoes for soup.

1. **Preposition of Source**

Preposition of source demonstrates the source of something or someone.

Examples:

- She was paid a scholarship by her college for all her semesters.
- All the love the child received was straight from his mother's heart.

1. **Preposition of Possession**

This preposition shows that something or someone belongs to something or someone. Such as of, with and to.

Some Examples

- I saw her with a black dress.
- This burger joint is of a well-known political leader.

Exercise 1. Fill up the blanks with suitable prepositions (about, at, by, for, from, in, of, on, to, with):

1. She learned Russianthe age of 45.
2. The book was writtenMark Twain.
3. I'll show you the picturethe palace.
4. We can only get to the campfoot.
5. He reminds me his old history teacher.
6. What are you talking?
7. the end of next year we will have made over £ 100,000.
8. She always gets up earlythe morning and goes to bed latenight.
9. I went to workTuesday but I didn't goFriday.
10. You'll have to wait. He'll be with youa minute.
11. Philip waitedher ....the movie theatre.

12. He started learning English2005.
13. You have to paythe tickets on the day you order them.
14. We are very proudthis company.
15. It's very kindyou to help us.
16. The old man suffereda heart attack.
17. Please writepencil.
18. It'stime you told him the truth.
19. The manager didn't take part the discussion.
20. He's very goodtelling jokes.
21. I'll see youthe conference
22. We sat downthe grass and ate our lunch.
23. My parents got marriedthe 1970s.
24. There's a good restaurantthe end of the street.
25. We usually have turkeyThanksgiving.
26. I would like to travelItaly next summer.
27. I took a plane Munich to Rome.
28. I'd like to speakthe manager please.
29. I don't usually feel tiredthe morning.
30. My mother is abroad so my dad is taking careusthe moment.
31. Sonja getsthe seven o'clock bus in the morning.
32. She always looksherself in the mirror.
33. I met Donnaa partyFriday night.
34. My friend always borrows moneyme.

1. The audience threw tomatoes him.
2. Passengers are not allowed to use cell phonesairplanes.
3. He is responsiblewhat he does.
4. I'm sorrythe job you didn't get.
5. I'm very badmathematics.
6. We had to climb slowlythe hill.
7. He is alwaystime.
8. How many people areyour team?
9. A university is where you studya degree.
10. Her next birthday will bea Sunday.
11. The new factory is expected to go onlineMay.

12. Many of us eatfork and spoon.
13. We have been searchinga web designer for a few weeks now.
14. The TV is the corner of the room.

• 161 •

CHAPTER NINE

Conjunction

Conjunction Definition

Conjunctions are very important words used in English. You use them every day! A Conjunction is a word that joins parts of a sentence, phrases or other words together. Conjunctions are used as single words or in pairs. Example: and, but, or are used by themselves, whereas, neither/nor, either/or are conjunction pairs.

Types of Conjunctions

1. **Coordinating conjunctions**– are single words that join similar words or phrases or elements.
2. **Subordinating conjunctions**– also join similar words, phrases or elements but exist in pairs.
3. **Correlative conjunctions**- They are actually adverbs that are used as conjunctions.

Examples of Conjunctions: FANBOYS

Let us now understand the use of different conjunctions that we routinely use in our day-to-day communication.

- For- It is used to sight a reason or purpose. *Example: I bought a new bag for my upcoming trip.*
- And- It connects or adds one thing to another. *Example: I love both apples and bananas.*
- Nor- It is used to indicate a negative idea to an already existing negative idea. *Example: Neither the white dress nor the yellow one looks good on me.*
- But- It is used to show a contrast between two items or ideas. *Example: I wanted to go for a hike but I have to go to work today.*
- Or- It is used to present an alternative to an already present positive idea. *Example: Would you like tea or coffee?*
- Yet- It is used to introduce an idea that adds something to a previous idea and is usually contrasting with it. *Example: I practice daily yet I couldn't put up a good show yesterday.*
- So- It is a conjunction that is used to indicate the effect or result of an occurrence. *Example: Both parents worked hard **so** that their children could study in good <u>schools</u>.*

All the above are coordinating conjunctions and are easy to remember using the pneumonic: '**FANBOYS**'. Coordinating conjunctions never come at the beginning of a sentence.

Some conjunctions, like the subordinating conjunctions, can come at the beginning of the sentence as well. They introduce a dependent <u>clause</u> and join it to an independent clause. Examples of this type of conjunction: *As, because, if, till, since,*and *when.* Few sentences that show the use of the above-mentioned conjunctions are:

- It is because of my parents that I can stand on my feet today.
- Life has not been the same since I fell for you.
- I'm sure of getting good grades because I study every day.

The third type of conjunctions i.e correlative conjunctions, as mentioned earlier in the chapter, are those which occur in pairs. They need to be used in the same sentence at different parts to make sense out of the sentence. Examples of these types of conjunction are: *Either: or, neither: nor, both: and, not only: but also, not: but* etc.

Few sentences that show the uses of the above-mentioned conjunctions are:

- You can *either* have the cheesecake *or* the frozen hot chocolate.
- She said she *neither* wanted the yogurt *nor* the ice cream.
- I am in the mood for *not* ice cream *but* for some waffles.

There are three more different types of conjunctions:

1. Coordinating Conjunctions:

Coordinating conjunction definition is as follows, the conjunction that joins two elements that have equal syntactic importance and grammatical rank. They can join two independent clauses, two phrases, two adjectives, two verbs or two nouns.

There are seven coordinating conjunctions, they are - for, and, nor, but, or, yet, and so. The easiest way to remember these conjunctions is with an acronym called FANBOYS.

Among all these conjunctions "so" can be used both as coordinating and subordinating conjunctions. As coordinating conjunction, it can link two independent clauses and as subordinate conjunction, it can link two unequal clauses.

Rules for using the Coordinating Conjunctions:

There are a few rules which have to be followed during the use of suitable conjunctions along with the usage of words in specific situations:

- When the coordinating conjunction connects two independent clauses, a comma has to be used before that conjunction.

  Example: I wanted to go shopping, but my friend wants to go to a movie.

- When coordinating conjunction is joining two phrases or words, a comma is not used before the conjunction.

  Example: I like to ride bikes and swim.

- A comma is optional when coordinating conjunction is used with more than two items.

2. Correlative Conjunctions:

These are a kind of tag-team conjunctions. They come in pairs where they are used in different places.
Correlative Conjunction Examples: either/or, neither/nor, not only/but also, whether/or, not/but.

- I either want a chocolate cake or pastry.
- She neither likes tea nor coffee.

3. Subordinating Conjunctions:

The subordinating conjunction meaning and examples are provided here. These are the types of conjunctions that help to join dependent clauses with independent clauses. Some of the common subordinating conjunctions are "since, because, though, as, although, while, and whereas". Sometimes the adverbs can also act as conjunctions such as, "until, after, or before".

Example: I can stay here until the clock strikes nine. Here the word "until" acts as a conjunction that connects two ideas such as, "can stay here" and "clock strikes nine". Here the first idea is independent of the second one hence, "can stay here" is an independent clause, and "clock strikes nine" is a dependent clause.

It is not mandatory to have the subordinating conjunctions in the middle of the sentence, but it has to be a part of the dependent clause. The dependent clause is also called the subordinate clause or subordinating sentences.

The dependent clause has two specific qualities,

- It cannot act as it's a sentence.
- It depends on the independent clause to provide a complete meaning.

Types of Subordinating Conjunctions

The subordinating conjunctions are categorized by meaning:

1. **Time:** When the main clause is performed or will be performed, the time-related conjunctions establish a period.

    Example: as soon as, once, before, still, whenever.
    I will clean the house after the relatives are gone.

1. **Concession:** By providing the additional information the concession conjunctions help to redefine the meaning of the main clause. It highlights the action that has happened in the hindrance or obstacle.

    Example: although, even though, as though.
    She wrote my article even though it is assigned to me.

1. **Comparison:** It helps to establish the connection between the words by providing a correlation.

   Example: though, whereas, just as, in contrast to.
   You will complete the work fastly whereas I need some more time.

1. **Cause:** It defines the reason the main clause was performed.

   Example: because, since, so that.
   My father always inspires me because he believes in me.

1. **Condition:** It provides the rules under which the main clause works.

   Example: If, in case, even if, unless.
   In case my sister suggests buying this dress, then I will go for it.

1. **Place:** It defines the place where the action or the activities occur.

   Example: wherever, whereas.
   I will place the conjunctions wherever it is necessary.

Conclusion

Here, we have seen the conjunction definition and examples, we can conclude that conjunctions help us to combine the simpler sentences to make a single complex sentence. We should be very careful while placing the comma and see to it that the appropriate conjunctions are used. The conjunctions that generally appear in the middle of the sentence are not preceded by the comma. If the subordinate clause appears at the starting of the sentence, then the whole sentence is followed by a comma.

Exercise 1. Complete each sentence using the <u>subordinating conjunction</u> from the parenthesis:

1. I visit the Grand Canyon __________ I go to Arizona. (once, whenever, wherever)
2. This is the place __________ we stayed last time we visited. (where, when, how)
3. __________ you win first place, you will receive a prize. (wherever, if, unless)
4. You won't pass the test __________ you study. (when, if, unless)
5. I could not get a seat, __________ I came early. (as, though, when)
6. We are leaving Wednesday __________ or not it rains. (if, whether, though)
7. Pay attention to your work __________ you will not make mistakes. (so that, unless, or)
8. The musicians delivered a rousing performance __________ they had rehearsed often. (though, as, once)
9. She's honest __________ everyone trusts her. (if, so, when)
10. Write this down __________ you forget. (or, when, lest)

Exercise 2. Complete each sentence using the correct <u>correlative conjunction</u> pair from the parenthesis:

1. I plan to take my vacation __________ in June __________ in July. (whether / or, either / or, as / if)
2. __________ I'm feeling happy __________ sad, I try to keep a positive attitude. (either / or, whether / or, when / I'm)
3. __________ had I taken my shoes off __________ I found out we had to leave again. (no sooner / than, rather / than, whether / or)
4. __________ only is dark chocolate delicious, __________ it can be healthy. (whether / or, not / but, just as / so)
5. __________ I have salad for dinner, __________________I can have ice cream for dessert. (if /then, when / than, whether

/ or)

6. ___________ flowers ___________ trees grow ___________ during warm weather. (not only / or, both / and, not / but)

7. ___________ do we enjoy summer vacation, ___________ we ___________ enjoy winter break. (whether / or, not only / but also, either / or)

8. Calculus is ___________ easy ___________ difficult ___________ (not / but, both / and, either / or)

9. It's ___________ going to rain ___________ snow tonight. (as / if, either / or, as / as)

10. Savory flavors are ___________ sweet ___________ sour. (often / and, neither / nor, both / and)

Exercise 3. Complete each sentence using the correct <u>coordinating conjunction</u> from the parenthesis:

1. My car has a radio ___________ a CD player. (but, or, and)

2. Sharon hates to listen to rap music, ___________ will she tolerate heavy metal. (but, nor, or)

3. Carol wanted to drive to Colorado, ___________ Bill insisted that they fly. (and, or, but)

4. I'm afraid of heights, ___________ I appreciate the view from the top of this building. (and, yet, nor)

5. I have to be on time, ___________ my boss will be annoyed if I'm late. (and, nor, for)

6. Do you like chocolate ___________ vanilla ice cream better? (or, nor, and)

7. I have to go to work at six, ___________ I'm waking up at four. (but, so, yet)

8. I was on time, ___________ everyone else was late. (so, but, for)

9. Nadia doesn't like to drive, ___________ she takes the bus everywhere. (but, yet, so)

10. Our trip to the museum was interesting, ___________ there were several new artifacts on display. (but, for, yet)

Exercise 4. Complete each sentence using the correct coordinating <u>conjunctive adverb</u> from the parenthesis:

1. Bianca wore her rain boots; __________, her feet stayed dry during the storm. (however, therefore, on the other hand)
2. I love the color red; __________, this shade seems a little too bright. (therefore, nonetheless, in fact)
3. You have to be on time; __________, you'll miss the train. (nonetheless, however, otherwise)
4. Teresa likes to read; __________, her sister Julia prefers to watch TV. (however, in contrast, again)
5. She really wanted to eat ice cream; __________, she had a salad. (however, likewise, instead)
6. We were working hard; __________, Jill and Jerry were lounging by the pool. (meanwhile, instead, therefore)
7. He is a weak leader; __________, he has plenty of supporters. (otherwise, moreover, nevertheless)
8. She has an incredible voice; __________, she will go far in her music career. (otherwise, undoubtedly, similarly)
9. Natalie wanted to make pie but didn't have apples; __________, she decided to bake a cake. (therefore, namely, in contrast)
10. We had hoped to go to Spain; __________, we ended up in France. (otherwise, instead, again)

Exercise 5. *Fill in the correct coordinating conjunction in the blank.*

1. Marsha doesn't play jazz.........the blues. She prefers hip-hop and rap.

1. John doesn't like chicken........does he like pork or burgers.

3. Sheila works hard,........she doesn't make a lot of money.

4. The sun is very strong,...........Jacob still won't wear any sunscreen.

5. I love you more than anything in the world,.........you are sweet and kind.

6. Would you like coffee............tea? I would prefer a cup of coffee.

7. Henry does not come from Mexico...........is from Belize. He is from Honduras.

8. I will go to Montreal............Quebec for the weekend. I'm not sure.

9. James is very tired,...........he will still come with us to the movies.

10. Wanda is very happy,...............she has finally earned her degree.

Exercise 6.*Fill in the blank using one of the subordinating conjunctions from the list. Use each word only once.*

1. I will never go to that restaurant again................I live.

2. ....Jose needs help, he calls his two brothers.

3. ....Sheldon works for the post office, he never works Sundays.

4. I would rather read a book.....................watch a stupid television program.

5. ....Roger goes to Miami, he will buy a new bathing suit.

6. ....travelers have time to pass through security, it is recommended that they

arrive two hours before their flight.

7. I will not go out with you...............you promise not to smoke

8. ....Maria is an avid jogger; her sister Julia prefers just to sit on the couch.

9. I do not believe..................Hector's father is a doctor.

10. Maryam loves the city.................she now lives.

Exercise 7. *Fill in the blank using one of the subordinating conjunctions from the list. Use each word only once.*

1. I would not see that movie........you gave me $100.

2. It is raining so hard............ the game was cancelled.

3. ....Sam was driving to school yesterday, he saw an accident.

4. I will love you..........the end of time.

5. ....he is the manager's son, he might still be fired because his work is so bad.

6. ....you need help, just call me.

7. ....Hank gets settled in, we will visit him.

8. I would like to drive.............take the bus.

9. I cannot go to that expensive restaurant...........you pay.

10. Leslie always drinks a cup of hot chocolate to relax her...........she goes to sleep.

CHAPTER TEN

Interjections

An interjection is one of the parts of speech used to express a particular emotion or sentiment (strong feeling or sudden emotion like surprise, joy, excitement, disgust, enthusiasm, sorrow, approval, calling, attention, etc) of the speaker to the reader. Interjection words are generally used at the beginning of a sentence. Sometimes, it is used as a single word or non-sentence phrase and followed by the punctuation mark.

Some other interjection words used as introductory expressions such as yes, no, well, indeed, etc. A comma (for a mild interjection) or an exclamation mark (for surprising, emotional, or deep feeling interjections) is used after the use of an interjection word in a sentence.

List/Words/Examples

Aah, Ahh, Aww, Bingo, Eh, Eww, Wow, Hey, Well, What, Hurrah, Hmph, Oh, Oops, Ouch, Shh, Uh oh, Whew, Yay/Yaay, Yeah, Yikes, Yippee, Uh, Hush, Hmmm, Er, Um, Bravo, Hello, Ugh, Ah, Ha ha, Well done, Alas, Fie, Hi, Yes, Ouch, Help, Happy Birthday, Good morning, dear, Hark, oops, huh, yum, oy, etc.

<u>For example:</u>

- **Good!** Now we can celebrate the party.
- **Oh,** what's a surprise.
- **Hey!** Get out of the building!

- **Yes**! I can do it easily.
- **No**! I run so long.
- **Well**! I have a good news.

Types of Interjection

Interjection is divided into the following types on the basis of ways to express interjections in the sentence such as greeting, joy, surprise, approval, sorrow, attention, and calling.

Interjections for Greeting

This type of interjection is used in the sentence to indicate the emotion of warmth to the person meeting with such as hey, hello, hi, etc.

For example:

- **Hey**! Nice to see you here in the party.
- **Hello**! I am Pooja.

Interjections for Joy

This type of interjection is used in the sentence to indicate immediate joy and happiness on any happy occasion that occurred such as hurrah, wow, hurray, etc.

For example:

- **Wow**! You are looking gorgeous.
- **Hurray**! We successfully won this football match.

Interjections for Approval

This type of interjection is used in the sentence to express the strong sense of approval or agreement for something that has happened such as well done, bravo, brilliant, etc.

For example:

Well done! You win the race.

Bravo! The first rank is yours this year.

Interjections for Attention

This type of interjection is used in the sentence to draw the attention of someone such as look, behold, listen, hush, etc.

For example:

- **Look**! You so arrogant.
- **Listen**! I have never copied you.
- **Behold**! Someone strange is there.

Interjections for Surprise

This type of interjection is used in the sentence to express the strong sense of surprise about something that has happened such as ha, what, hey, ah, oh, eh, etc.

For example:

- **What**! You failed.
- **Oh**! Really you completed the task, I can't believe.
- **Ah**! I got new job.

Interjections for Sorrow

This type of interjection is used in the sentence to express the emotion of sadness about something unfortunate that has happened such as alas, ouch, ah, oh, etc.

For example:

- **Alas**! He is no more.
- **Ouch**! It's very paining.

Interjections for Understanding/Misunderstanding

Interjections of understanding and misunderstanding are used to express one's understanding of a subject being talked about or something which wasn't well understood before the moment.

Other Interjections

(Interjections of Anger/Annoyance/Frustration/ Disappointment/Dismissive)

Apart from the Interjections that we have studied in the preceding chapters, there are many other Interjections that are used to express different kinds of emotions.

Exercise 1. add to the below sentences the appropriate kind of Interjections from the choices given and also state the emotion they are expressing. Please assess your progress by referring to the Answer provided at the end of the exercise.

1) _______! The train stopped again!

a) Aww

b) Argh

c) Hi

2) _______! I will not let him go without an explanation!

a) Grr

b) Hah

c) Duh

3) _______! I didn't intend to harm you!

a) Oops

b) Hey

c) Phew

4) _________! It missed with a flicker!

a) Aww

b) Aha

c) Phew

5) _______! Did you hear that!

a) Uh oh

b) Ssh

c) Umm

6) _______! It's pricking my ear!

a) Aah

b) Hey

c) Yahoo

7) _______! I would have never done that anyways!

a) Grr

b) Bah

c) Boo hoo

8) ___________! I broke my knee!

a) Yippee

b) Yahoo

c) Boo hoo

9) _________! Such a nice baby!

a) Ouch

b) Aww

c) Oops

10) _________! A snake!

a) Eek

b) Grr

c) Hah

11) _________! To our next match!

a) Cheers

b) Boo hoo

c) Bah

12) _________! I didn't realize the consequences!

a) Ssh

b) Grr

c) Gosh

13) _________! That was a funny joke!

a) Yippee

b) Ha ha

c) My God

14) _________! Give me a moment!

a) Yikes

b) Hmm

c) Holy cow

15) _________! The whole vessel just went down!

a) Duh

b) Yeek

c) Holy smoke

16) _________! It's freezing outside!

a) Brrr

b) Eek

c) Oops

17) _________! Is anybody home?

a) yahoo

b) Cheers

c) Hello

18) ______! I don't like cockroaches!

a) Eww

b) Fuff

c) Boo

19) _________! What nonsense!

a) Ahem

b) Hurrah

c) Fuff

20) _________! Scared you!

a) Yippee

b) Booh

c) Bingo

21) _________! It's smelling foul!

a) Oh

b) Ouch

c) Yuck

22) _________! Go away!

a) Hi

b) Shoo

c) Hello

23) _________! I think we are out of fuel.

a) Uh oh

b) Duh

c) Gosh

24) __________ ! We made it!

a) Oops

b) Hurray

c) Yikes

25) _________! You did it son!

a) bravo

b) Umph

c) Duh

26) _________! Why are you wearing this jacket in summer!

a) hurrah

b) Yippee

c) Good grief

27) _________! You are all wet!

a) Eew

b) Oh dear

c) Oops

28) _________! It hurts!

a) Eww

b) Ouch

c) Duh

29) _______! Did it hurt!

a) Oops

b) Argh

c) Urgh

30) _______! I didn't do that!

a) yahoo

b) Yippee

c) Nuh

Exercise 2. Fill up the blanks with suitable interjections:

1. .... Thank God!

2. .... I didn't see you were hiding here.

3. .... I'll help you.

4. .... We have won the match.

5. .... I felt bad hearing that.

6. .... Now that's what I call a good shot

7. .... That show was so gory.

8. .... Don't make a noise.

9. .... I can't believe you lost my favourite book,

10. .... what did he say?

Exercise 3. Make appropriate sentences using the following interjections.

1. Alas
2. Yeah,
3. Great
4. Eh!
5. Ugh!
6. Stop!
7. Wow!
8. Yes!
9. What!

Exercise 4. Fill the blanks with the appropriate interjection.

1. __________ What are you doing there?
2. __________ He is dead.
3. __________ We have won the game.
4. __________ Have they gone?
5. __________ I got such a fright.
6. __________ Don't make noise.
7. __________ you've stepped on my toes.
8. __________ I've got a toothache.
9. What do you think of that, __________
10. Kathmandu is the capital of ,__________ ,Nepal.
11. __________ that seems nice.
12. "It's hot today." "__________?" "I said it's hot today."
13. __________ What a great idea!
14. __________ please say 'yes'!
15. __________ look at that!
16. __________ I don't think that's a good idea.
17. __________ Sia is here!
18. __________ I don't know the answer to that.
19. Shall we go? __________
20. 98 divided by 7 is ___ 14.

CHAPTER ELEVEN

Tense

Tenses denote the time of action. They show when the work is done. They are:

1. Present Tense
2. Past Tense
3. Future Tense

They are further divided into:

1. *__Simple Present-__*It is used to denote scientific facts, universal truths and work done on daily basis.

   Assertive Rule: Subject+ V^1-s/es+ Object
   Example,
   She writes a letter.
   They play hockey.
   Negative Rule: Subject+ do not/does not + V^1 + Object
   Examplc,
   They do not go there.
   He doesn't play cricket.
   Interrogative Rule: Do/Does + Subjects + V^1+ Object
   Example,
   Does he eat banana?
   Do they take care of their parents?

INTERROGATIVE NEGATIVE ASSERTIVE --- Does + sub + not + v1 + s/es + object
Example – Does she not write a letter?

1. ***Present Continuous*** – It is used to express an action taking place at the time of speaking.

    ASSERTIVE RULE --- sub + is/am/are + v1 + ing + object
    Example – she is writing a letter.
    NEGATIVE RULE --- sub + is/am/are + not + v1 + ing + object
    Example – She is not writing a letter.
    INTERROGATIVE RULE --- is/am/are + sub + v1 + ing + object
    Example – Is she writing a letter?
    INTERROGATIVE NEGATIVE RULE --- is/am/are + sub + not + v1 + ing + object
    Example – Is she not writing a letter?

1. ***Present Perfect*** – It is used to show an action that started in the past and has just finished.

    ASSERTIVE RULE --- sub + has/have + v3 + object
    Example- She has written a letter.
    NEGATIVE RULE --- sub + has/have + not + v3 + object
    Example – She has not written a letter.
    INTERROGATIVE RULE --- has/have + sub + v3 + object
    Example- Has she written a letter?
    INTERROGATIVE NEGATIVE RULE ---has/have + sub + not + v3 + object
    Example– Has she not written a letter?

3. ***Present Perfect Continuous*** – This tense shows the action which started in the past and is still continuing.

    ASSERTIVE RULE --- sub + has/have + been + v1 + ing + object
    Example – She has been writing a letter.

NEGATIVE RULE --- sub + has/have + not been + v1 + ing + object

Example– She has not been writing a letter.

INTERROGATIVE RULE ---has/have + sub + been + v1 + ing + object

Example – Has she been writing a letter?

INTERROGATIVE NEGATIVE RULE --- has/have + she + not + been + v1 + ing + object

Example – Has she not been writing a letter?

<u>Past Tense</u>

Tense symbolizes the ever moving, non-stop wheel of time which is forever busy gathering moments of future and throwing them into the dustbin of past

<u>Simple Past</u>

Used to indicate an action completed in the past. It often occurs with adverb of time. Sometimes it is used without an adverb of time.

Used for past habits.

Eg. I played football when I was a child. Rule: **Subject + V2**

Eg She wrote a letter

1. Assertive Sentences – **Subject + V2 + Object + (.)** She wrote a letter.

2. Negative Sentences-

Subject + didn't + V1 + Object + (.)

She didn't.write a letter.

3. Interrogative Sentences-

Did + Subject + V1 + Object + (?)

Did she write a letter?

   4. Interrogative Negative Sentences-

Did + Subject + not + V1 + Object + (?)

Did she not write a letter?
Past Continuous Tense
Used to denote an action going on at some time in the past.
e.g. I was driving a car. Rule: was/were + ing

   1. Assertive Sentences –

Subject + was/were +V1+ ing + Object + (.)

She was writing a letter.

   2. Negative Sentences-

Subject + was/were + not + ing + Object + (.)

She was not writing a letter.

   3. Interrogative Sentences-

Was/were + Subject + ing+ Object + (?)

Was she writing a letter?

   4. Interrogative Negative Sentences-

Was/were + Subject + not + ing+ Object + (?)

Was she not writing a letter?

<u>Past Perfect Tense</u>

Used to describe an action completed before a certain moment in the past, usually a long time ago. If two actions happened in the past, past perfect is used to show the action that took place earlier.

e.g. The patient had died before the doctor came.

1. Assertive Sentences –

Subject + had + V3 + Object + (.)

She had written a letter.

2. Negative Sentences-

Subject + had + not + Object + (.)

She had not written a letter.

3. Interrogative Sentences-

Had + Subject + V3 + Object ⏐ (?)

Had she written a letter?

4. Interrogative Negative Sentences-

Had + Subject + not + V3 + Object + (?)

Had she not written a letter?
Past Perfect Continuous Tense
Used to denote an action that began before a certain point in the past and continued up to some time in past.

e.g. I had been learning English in this school for 20 days.

1. Assertive Sentences –

Subject + had been +V1 + ing + Object + (.)

She had been writing a letter.

2. Negative Sentences-

Subject + had + not been + V1+ ing + Object + (.)

She had not been writing a letter.

3. Interrogative Sentences-

Had + Subject+ been+ V1 + ing + Object + (?)

Had she been writing a letter?

4. Interrogative Negative Sentences-

Had + Subject +not + been + V1 + ing + Object + (?)

Had she not been writing a letter?

FUTURE TENSE

Time and tide wait for no man. So, a period of time following the moment of speaking or writing is called as future tense.

For e.g- She will write a letter.

Simple Future

This tense tells us about an action which has not occurred yet and will occur after saying or in future

Rule – **Will/Shall + Verb (Ist form)**

In Future Tense helping verb 'Shall' is used with 'I' and 'We'. Helping verb 'Will' is used with all others. When you are to make a commitment or warn someone or emphasize something, use of 'will/shall' is reversed. 'Will' is used with 'I' & 'We' and 'shall' is used with others.

In general speaking there is hardly any difference between 'shall & will' and normally 'Will' is used with all.

Now, let us use this rule in various forms of sentences;

1. Positive / Affirmative Sentences –

    Subject + Will/Shall + Verb (Ist form) + Object + (.)
    She will write a letter.

2. Negative Sentences-

    Subject + Will/Shall + Not + Verb (Ist form) + Object + (.)
    She will not write a letter.

3. Interrogative Sentences-

    Will/Shall + Subject + Verb (Ist form) + Object + (?)
    Will she write a letter?

4. Interrogative Negative Sentences-

Will/Shall + Subject + Not + Verb (Ist form) + Object + (?)
Will she not write a letter?
<u>Future Continuous Tense</u>
It is used to express an ongoing or continued action in future.

e.g. He will be distributing sweets in temple tomorrow at 12 o'clock.

In the example, the action will start in future (tomorrow) and action is thought to be continued till sometime in future.

We use the future continuous to talk about something that will be in progress at or around a time in the future.

Rule: **Will/Shall + Be + Verb (Ist form) + Ing**

Now, let us use this rule in various forms of sentences;

1. Positive / Affirmative Sentences –

Subject + Will/Shall + Be + Verb (Ist form) + Ing + Object + (.)
She will be writing a letter.

2. Negative Sentences-

Subject + Will/Shall + Not + Be + Verb (Ist form) + Ing + Object + (.)
She will not be writing a letter.

3. Interrogative Sentences-

Will/Shall + Subject + Be + Verb (Ist form) + Ing + Object + (?)
Will she be writing a letter?

4. Interrogative Negative Sentences-

Will/Shall + Subject + Not + Be + Verb (Ist form) + Ing + Object + (?)
Will she not be writing a letter?
<u>Future Perfect Tense</u>

It is used to express an action which will happen/occur in future and will be completed by a certain time in future.

We use the future perfect to say that something will be finished by a particular time in the future.

e.g. They will have shifted the house by Sunday morning. Rule: **Will/Shall + Have + Verb (3rd form)**

Now, let us use this rule in various forms of sentences;

1. Positive / Affirmative Sentences –

Subject + Will/Shall + Have + Verb (3rd form) + Object + (.)
She will have written a letter.

2. Negative Sentences-

Subject + Will/Shall + Not + Have + Verb (3rd form) + Object + (.)
She will not have written a letter.

3. Interrogative Sentences-

Will/Shall + Subject + Have + Verb (3rd form) + Object + (?)
Will she have written a letter?

4. Interrogative Negative Sentences-

Will/Shall + Subject + Not + Have + Verb (3rd form) + Object + (?)
Will she not have written a letter?

Future Perfect Continuous Tense

It is used to talk about actions that will commence at a fix time in future and will continue for some time in future.

If there is no time reference, then it is not a Future perfect continuous tense. Without continued time reference, such sentences are Future Continuous Tense. Continued time reference only differentiates between Future Continuous Tense and Future Perfect Continuous Tense.

The future perfect progressive emphasize the duration of an activity that will be in progress before another time or event in the future.

e.g. This time tomorrow, I will be enjoying the cricket match in the stadium. It is also used to talk about planned actions or actions expected to happen.

e.g. They will be staying for a week's

The future perfect progressive emphasize the duration of an activity that will be in progress before another time or event in the future.

Rule: **Will/Shall + Have been + Verb (Ist form) + Ing**

Now, let us use this rule in various forms of sentences;

1. Positive / Affirmative Sentences –

Subject + Will/Shall + Have been + Verb (Ist form) + Ing + Object + (.)

She will have been writing a letter.

2. Negative Sentences-

Subject + Will/Shall + Not + Have been + Verb (Ist form) + Ing + Object+ (.)

She will not have been writing a letter.

3. Interrogative Sentences-

Will/Shall + Subject + Have been + Verb (Ist form) + Ing + Object +(?)

Will she have been writing a letter?

4. Interrogative Negative Sentences-

Will/Shall + Subject + Not + Have been + Verb (Ist form) + Ing + Object +(?)

Will she not have been writing a letter?

Exercise 1. Fill in the correct form of the verb – All tenses

1. My family have(_**buy**_) some land in southern France recently. They

   (_**build**_) a summer house there at the moment.

2. Andy and Mary(_**go**_) to a concert tomorrow night. They

   (_**look forward to**_) it the whole week.

3. Jonathon(_**watch**_) the news on TV every day and it (_**help**_) him with his English.

4. My car(_**break**_) down when I(_**drive**_) home from work. I(_**fix**_) it if I(_**know**_) what was wrong. But I didn't so(_**have**_) to take it to the garage.

5. When he(_**found**_) Microsoft, Bill Gates was only 20 years old. He

   (_**already write**_) his first computer programme six years earlier.

6. An accident(_**happen**_) near my house last night. A car (_**hit**_) a young man. He(_**ride**_) his bike when someone in front of him suddenly(_**open**_) a car door. Many people(_**see**_) the accident. The police(_**interrogate**_) them last night.

7. Mrs Smith said that one day she(_**retire**_) from teaching. She said that she(_**spend**_) her new free time learning about computers.

8. I_ (_**not sleep**_) at all last night. Someone(_**listen**_) to music all night.

9. I(_**see**_) a film a week ago, but I(_**not enjoy**_) it very much because I_ (_**already read**_) the book. If I

(***not read***) the book I_ (***probably enjoy***) the film more.

10. The judge sentenced the man to eight years in prison because he(***rob***) a bank.
11. They(***stand***) in the queue for over an hour when the manager

    (***tell***) them that there were no more tickets.

12. Alan(***be***) in the car accident yesterday. The other driver

    (***lose***) control of his car because he(***fall***) asleep.

13. She(***not see***) her father since he(***start***) to work in Marseille two years ago.
14. I(***sleep***) when the fire broke out.
15. Linda phoned and explained that she(***not can***) to come to the party the next day because she(***be***) still sick.
16. I(***just see***) the film "The Da Vinci Code". – (***you see***) it too? – No, I(***not have***) but I(***read***) the book.
17. My sister(***fly***) home from London today. Her flight (***arrive***) in an hour so I(***leave***) for the airport right now to get there in time.
18. Unless he(***sell***) more he won't get much money.
19. While he(***wait***) for the bus there(***be***) a robbery at the bank. After the robbers(***go***) away the police (***come***) but they(***not can***) to catch them.

CHAPTER TWELVE

Direct and Indirect Speech

Direct and indirect speech are two ways of reporting a statement made by a speaker. Learn the definition, rules, and examples of direct and indirect speech, as well as how to convert direct speech into indirect speech. *Updated: 01/11/2022*

Background on Communication

Spoken and written communication is like one big game of telephone. Sometimes we hear the original tale, and other times we hear a retelling of the story. In this lesson, we're going to explore what that means by studying the difference between direct and indirect speech and learning proper grammar techniques for both.

Direct Speech

Direct speech, also known as quoted speech, consists of words or phrases that are taken directly from the source. These words are quoted or written exactly as the words were originally spoken.

With regard to direct speech, there is no interpretation or annotation; the words are taken directly from one source and repeated to another. In other words, we take the words directly from the speaker and repeat them exactly as they were originally stated.

Here are some examples of direct speech:

- Jonah said, "I don't like your hat."
- Jonah said, "Please take off that Yankees hat."
- Jane said, "It's not my fault that you are a Red Sox fan."

In these examples, the direct speech is shown in quotations, which signifies that the speech is taken directly from the source with no alterations.

Indirect Speech

Indirect speech, also known as reported speech, is when words or phrases are reported in our own words. The original words are modified and/or interpreted as opposed to being quoted.

When talking about indirect speech, we use words that refer to something that has already happened. To do so, we are speaking in the past tense and are summarizing, modifying, or synthesizing what has already been said.

Here are some examples of indirect speech:

- Amy said it was cold.
- He said he had been on Facebook since 2010.
- She said she had been teaching college classes for two years.

Converting Direct to Indirect Speech

When we use direct speech, we are repeating what was said. When we use indirect speech, we're reporting what was said. Let's now look at some specific examples to learn how to change speech from direct to indirect. These examples will also reinforce the difference between direct and indirect speech.

1. Changing From Present Tense to Past Tense

When converting speech from direct to indirect, you must change the present tense verbs to the past tense and remove any quotation marks or commas.

Direct Speech (Present Tense)

Indirect Speech (Past Tense)

Jenn says, "I love watching TV."

Jenn said she loved watching TV.

2. Changing From Simple Past Tense to Past Perfect Tense

What if the direct speech is already written in the past tense? If the sentence is written in simple past tense, you just remove the punctuation and change the verb to past perfect to make it indirect speech.

Direct Speech (Simple Past Tense)

Indirect Speech (Past Perfect Tense)

Lana said, "I saw him at the mall."

Lana said she had seen him at the mall.

3. Changing Speech in the Form of a Question

What if direct speech is in the form of a question? For example: "Do you want to go on a trip to Europe?" To make a direct question indirect, follow the same tense change rules as before, add "asked me" to signify reporting a question, and keep the question word.

To unlock this lesson you must be a Study.com Member. <u>Create your account</u>

Additional Activities

Direct v. Indirect Speech: Activities

Lesson Comprehension Questions

Which of the following is *not* an attribute of direct speech?

- Direct speech reports exactly what was said.
- Direct speech includes the writer's interpretation or paraphrase of what someone has said.
- Direct speech includes quotation marks.

Which of the following is *not* an attribute of indirect speech?

- Indirect speech is also called reported speech.

- Indirect speech usually includes the past tense indicating that something has previously happened.
- Indirect speech is necessarily biased.

Which of the following is *not* the correct shift in tense from direct speech to indirect speech?

- Simple present tense --> simple past tense
- Simple past tense --> past perfect tense
- Simple present tense --> simple future tense

Direct Speech to Indirect Speech
Change the sentences including direct speech below to indirect speech.

- Caroline said, "I enjoyed birdwatching."
- Tyler reports, "Los Angeles continues to suffer from a severe drought."
- She asked, "Can you help me inflate the tire in my bicycle."
- (Request from Jeremy to Susan) "Pick up the trash."
- I asked, "Do you like chocolate milk?"
- She explained, "He already read *Jane Eyre*."
- (Avery asks Rebecca) "Are there any good hiking trails?"

Reported Speech is also known as Direct and Indirect Speech or Narration. In Indirect Speech, we convey the speaker's message in our own words. Thus, the message can be conveyed in 2 ways.

1. Direct Speech
2. Indirect Speech

Direct speech is known as repeating the exact words spoken and Indirect speech is known as reporting the words.

But the question occurs how to report or how to use Indirect speech? There are certain rules to make changes in a sentence from

Direct to Indirect speech. Read the complete blog to know more.

Direct and Indirect Speech Rules

Below, we are sharing the rules to make changes from Direct to Indirect speech. The changes of Direct and Indirect speech depend on some factors like modals, reporting verb, place, time, tense, pronoun etc. You can check the complete information of changes in Direct and Indirect speech.

Direct Speech

Indirect Speech

Can

Could

May

Might

Must

Had to/ Would have to

Should

Should

Might

Might

Could

Could

Would

Would

Ought to

Ought to

<u>*Direct and Indirect Speech Exercises for Modals:*</u>

Look to the Direct and Indirect Speech examples with answers using modals.

1. He said, "I can cook food."

He said that he could cook food.

1. They said, "We may go to Canada."

   They said that they might go to Canada.

3. She said, "I must finish the work on time."

   She said that she had to finish the work on time.
   Modals that remain unchanged are: Should, might, could, would, ought to.

4. Kanika said, "I ought to avoid junk food."

   Kanika said that she ought to avoid junk food.

Changes as per Reporting Verb

According to the reporting verb, changes are made in the direct sentence or the sentence in inverted commas.

If the reporting verb is in the past tense, then the direct sentence is changed in its past tense.

The tense of direct speech remains unchanged when the reporting verb is in the present or future tense.

If the direct sentence contains the universal truth, then it remains unchanged in the Indirect Speech.

<u>*Direct and Indirect Speech Exercises for Reporting Verb*</u>

Below, we are providing Direct and Indirect Speech examples using reporting verb changes.

1. Navin said, "He is young."

Navin said that he was young.

2. Isha says, "I am pretty."

Isha says that she is pretty.

3. Rohan will say, "I am tall."

Rohan will say that he is tall.

4. They said, "The sun rises in the east."

They said that the sun rises in the east.

Changes as per Tense

In the below table, we are sharing how tense changes into Indirect speech.

Direct Speech
Indirect Speech
Present simple
(Subject +V1st + Object)
Past simple
(Subject +V2 + Object)
Present continuous
(Subject +is/am/are+V1 +ing+ Object)
Past Continuous
(Subject +was/were+V1 +ing+ Object)
Present perfect
(Subject + has/have+V3+Object)
Past perfect
(Subject+had+V3+Object)
Past simple
(Subject+V2+Object)
Past perfect

(Subject+had+V3+Object)
Past Continuous
(Subject +was/were+V1 +ing+ Object)
Past perfect continuous
(Subject +had been+V1 +ing+ Object)
Future simple
(Subject+ will/shall+V1+object)
Present Conditional
(Subject+ would+V1+object)
Future Continuous
(Subject +will/shall+be+V1 +ing+ Object)
Conditional Continuous
(Subject +would+be+V1 +ing+ Object)

Direct and Indirect speech exercises for Tense

Check the Direct and Indirect speech examples for tense using the above table. Changes will always be made according to the given table only.

1. Heena said, "I walk."

    Heena said that she walked.

2. Deepak said, "I am having tea."

    Deepak said that he was having tea.

3. Ayesha said, "Honey has left for school."

    Ayesha said that Honey had left for school.

4. Vidisha said, "Ananya took pasta."

Vidisha said that Ananya had taken pasta.

5. They told, "We were living in Paris."

They told that they had been living in Paris.

6. Ramesh said, "I will go to Sri Lanka."

Ramesh said that he would go to Sri Lanka.

7. Aishwarya Said, "They will be watering plants."

Aishwarya said that they would be watering plants.

Changes in Place and Time

Words are changed in an Indirect Speech to replace nearness from distance. In the table, we are sharing some words which are changed in Indirect speech.

Direct Speech
Indirect Speech
Now
Then
Here
There
Today
That day
Tomorrow
The next day
Last week
The previous week
This
That
Tonight
That night

Ago

Before

Thus

So

Hither

Thither

Come

Go

Hence

Thence

Next

Following

Changes of Interrogative Sentences

Here, we are sharing certain rules of Direct and Indirect speech for interrogative sentences conversions.

The reporting verb said/said to is changed in asked, demanded, ordered, enquired as per the nature of the sentence.

While a sentence starts with reporting verb then at the conversion time if /whether is used as the joining clause.

In case the sentence starts from "Wh" question word, then no extra conjunction is used.

<u>Direct and Indirect Speech Exercises for Interrogative Sentences</u>

We are applying the above rules in the given exercise below to make changes in Direct and Indirect speech.

1. Ravi said, "What is Heena doing?"

    Ravi asked me what Heena was doing.

2. Esha said, "Will she come for lunch?"

Esha asked if she would come for lunch.

3. The boy asked, "Where do you stay?"

The boy inquired where I stayed

Changes of Pronouns

While making the changes from Direct and Indirect speech, one should be having knowledge of rules of changes in pronouns.

The first person in reported speech changes according to the subject of reporting speech.

In Reported Speech change of the second person depends on the object of reporting speech.

The third person remains unchanged.

You can check the table for the changes in pronoun.

Direct Speech

Indirect Speech

I

He/she

You

He/she/they

We

They

They

They

He

He

She

She

It

It

Us

Them

Our

Their

His

His

Her

Her

Its

Its

Direct and Indirect Speech Exercises for Changes in Pronoun

1. Vidya said, "I am a good girl."

Vidya said that she was a good girl.

2. I told them, "You have finished your work."

I told them that they had finished their work.

3. He said, "She is in Delhi."

He said that she was in Delhi.

Exercise 1. Change these sentences into Indirect Speech:

1. John said to me," When you came here, it was raining."
2. Sam says," Everyday I read this book to get knowledge."
3. Tom said to Mary," Don't take me for granted."
4. She said," Well, I can do this work."
6. She said to me," Happy birthday to you."
7. I said to him," You fool!"
8. The master said to his servant," Don't bring me tea now."
9. The PM said to the countrymen," Make the country clean."
10. I said to him," Let us go for walk."
. My brother told me," You are lazy."
12. "Why don't you consult the doctor?", he said to me

13. They say to us," We have been living here for two years."

14. Doctor said to him, " Play everyday to be fit and keep away the diseases."

15. Shobha said, " I listen to music in the morning everyday. "

Exercise 2. Change the following sentences into Indirect Speech:

1. She said to me," I like you very much."
2. I said to her," Why do you like me?"
3. Rudra said to Kinjal," Are you stupid?"
4. Kinjal said to her father," Bring me a car."
5. John said to me," Do you know where he is?"
6. She said," What a tall boy you are!"
7. The students said," Alas! We are failed again."
8. Kinjal said," Hurrah! I have won the scholarship "
9. The teacher says," Rose smells sweet."
10. I said to him, "When I went there, he was sleeping."
11. She said to me, "I had been waiting for you for two hours."
12. I said," Well, you have completed this task."
13. Jessy said to Harley," May I borrow your book?"
14. I said to my teacher," Good morning, sir."
15. Mona said to me," You know me, don't you?"

Exercise 3. Change these sentences into Direct Speech:

1. She said (that) he worked in a bank.
2. She told me (that) they went (had gone) out last night (the night before).
3. She said (that) she was coming
4. She told me (that) she was waiting for the bus whenhe arrived.
5. She said (that) she hadnever been there before.
6. She told me (that) she didn't go (hadn't gone) to the party.
7. 7.She said (that) Lucy wouldcome later.

8. She told me (that) he hadn't eaten breakfast.
9. She said (that) she could help me tomorrow.

10. She told me (that) I should go to bed early.
11. She told me (that) she didn't like chocolate.
12. She said (that) she wouldn't see me tomorrow.
13. She said (that) she is living in Paris for a few months.
14. She told me (that) she visited (had visited) her parents at the weekend.
15. She said (that) she hadn't eaten sushi before.
16. She said (that) she hadn't travelled by underground before she came to London.
17. She said (that) they would help if they could.
18. She told me (that) she would do the washing-up later.
19. She said (that) he could read when he was three.
20. She said (that) she had been sleeping when Julie called.

Exercise 4. Change these statements into Direct Speech:

1. She asked me where hewas.
2. She asked me what I was doing.
3. She asked me why I went (had gone) out last night.
4. She asked me who that beautiful woman was.
5. She asked me how my mother was.
6. She asked me what I was going to do at the weekend.
7. She asked me where I would live after graduation.
8. She asked me what I had been doing when she saw (had seen) me.
9. She asked me how the journey was (had been).
10. She asked me how often I went to the cinema.
11. She asked me if I lived in London.
12. She asked me if he arrived (had arrived) on time.
13. She asked me if I had been to Paris.
14. She asked me if I could help her.
15. She asked me if I was working tonight (that night).
16. She asked me if I would come later.
17. She asked me if I liked coffee.
18. She asked me if this was the road to the station.

19. She asked me if I did (had done) my homework.
20. She asked me if I had studied.

Exercise 5. Change the following statements into Direct Speech:

1. She asked me to help her carry that.
2. She asked me to come early.
3. She asked me to buy some milk.
4. She asked me to open the window.
5. She asked me to bring the book tonight (that night).
6. She asked me to help her with her homework.
7. She asked me to bring her a cup of coffee.
8. She asked me to pass the salt.
9. She asked me to lend her a pencil.
10. She asked me to tell her the time.
11. She told me to do my homework.
12. She told me to go to bed.
13. She told me not to be late.
14. She told me not to smoke.
15. She told me to tidy my room.
16. She told me to wait here (there).
17. She told me not to do that.
18. She told me to eat my dinner.
19. She told me not to make a mess.
20. She told me to do the washing-up.

CHAPTER THIRTEEN

Active and Passive Voice

Active and Passive Voice Rules for All Tenses

Here, we are listing out the Active and Passive Voice Rules for all tenses. You will come to know how an auxiliary verb is used to change a sentence from Active to Passive voice.

Active and Passive Voice Rules for Present Simple Tense

Here in this table, we are elaborating Rules of Active and Passive Voice with examples for Present Simple.

Active Voice
Passive Voice
(Auxiliary Verb – is/am/are)
Subject + V1+s/es+ object
Object+ is/am/are+ V3+ by + subject
Subject + Do/does+ not + V1 + Object
Object + is/am/are+ not + V3+ by Subject
Does+ Subject+ V1+Object+?
Is/am/are + Object+ V3+ by subject +?
Active and Passive Voice Example with Answers of Present Simple Tense
Active: He reads a novel.
Passive: A novel is read.

Active: He does not cook food.

Passive: Food is not cooked by him.

Active: Does he purchase books?

Passive: Are books purchased by him?

Active: They grow plants.

Passive: Plants are grown by them.

Active: She teaches me.

Passive: I am taught by her.

Active and Passive Voice Rules for Present Continuous Tense

Below we will explain the Rules of Active and Passive Voice with examples for Present Continuous tense.

Active Voice

Passive Voice

(Auxiliary Verb- is/am/are + being)

Subject + is/am/are+ v1+ ing + object

Object+ is/am/are+ being+ V3+ by + subject

Subject + is/am/are+ not+ v1+ ing+ object

Object + is/am/are+ not + being+V3+ by Subject

Is/am/are+ subject+v1+ing + object+?

Is/am/are + Object+ V3+ by subject +?

Active and Passive Voice Exercises of Present Continuous Tense

Active: Esha is singing a song.

Passive: A song is being sung by Esha.

Active: Kritika is not chopping vegetables.

Passive: Vegetables are not being chopped by Kritika.

Active: Is Ritika buying a table?

Passive: Is a table being bought by Ritika?

Active: They are serving poor people.

Passive: Poor people are being served by them.

Active: She is disturbing Dinesh.

Passive: Dinesh is being disturbed by her.

Active and Passive Voice Rules for Present Perfect Tense

Active Voice
Passive Voice
(Auxiliary Verb- has/have +been)
Subject + has/have+ v3+ object
Object+ has/have+ been+ V3+ by + subject
Subject + has/have+ not+ v3+ object
Object + has/have+ not + been+V3+ by Subject
Has/have+ subject+ v3 + object+?
Has/Have + Object+ been+V3+ by subject +?
You can understand passive voice for present perfect tense from the list which are given below.

Active and Passive Voice Example with Answers of Present Perfect Tense
Active: Nitesh has challenged her.
Passive: She has been challenged by Nitesh.
Active: Radhika has not written an article.
Passive: An article has not been written by Radhika.
Active: Have they left the apartment?
Passive: Has apartment been left by them?
Active: She has created this masterpiece.
Passive: This masterpiece has been created by her.
Active: I have read the newspaper.
Passive: The newspaper has been read by me.

Active and Passive Voice Rules for Past Simple Tense

Here in the below table, you can check Active and Passive Voice Rules for past simple tense.
Active Voice
Passive Voice

(Auxiliary Verb- was/were)

Subject + V2+ object

Object+ was/were V3+ by + subject

Subject +did+ not+v1+ object

Object + was/were+ not +V3+ by Subject

Did+ subject+V1+ object+?

Was/were + Object+ V3+ by subject +?

Active and Passive Voice Exercises of Past Simple Tense

Active: Reema cleaned the floor.

Passive: The floor was cleaned by Reema.

Active: Aisha bought a bicycle.

Passive: A bicycle was bought by Aisha.

Active: Naman called my friends.

Passive: My friends were called by Naman.

Active: I saved him.

Passive: He was saved by me.

Active: Miraya paid the bills.

Passive: The bills were paid by Miraya.

Active and Passive Voice Rules forPast Continuous Tense

We can easily convert sentences from Active to Passive Voice according to given rules below.

Active Voice

Passive Voice

(Auxiliary Verb- was/were + being)

Subject + was/were + v1+ing+ object.

Object+ was/were +being+V3+ by + subject

Subject +was/were+ not+v1+ing + object

Object + was/were+ not +being+V3+ by Subject

Was/were+ Subject + V1+ing + object+?

Was/were + Object+ being+v3+ by+ subject+?

Active and Passive Voice Examples with Answers of Past Continuous Tense

Active: Nitika was painting the wall.

Passive: The wall was being painted by Nitika.

Active: Manish was repairing the car.

Passive: The car was being repaired by Manish.

Active: Were you reciting the poem?

Passive: Was the poem being recited?

Active: She was baking the cake.

Passive: The cake was being baked by her.

Active: She was watching me.

Passive: I was being watched by her.

Active and Passive Voice Rules forPast Perfect Tense

There are certain Active and Passive Voice Rules for Past perfect tense, with these only you can convert any sentence in Passive Voice.

Active Voice

Passive Voice

(Auxiliary Verb- had +been)

Subject + had + v3+ object.

Object+ had+been +V3+ by + subject

Subject +had+ not+v3+ object

Object + had+ not +been+V3+ by Subject

Had+ Subject + V3+ object+?

Had + Object+ been+v3+ by+ subject+?

Active and Passive Voice Exercises of Past Perfect Tense

Active: Misha had cleaned the floor.

Passive: The floor had been cleaned by Misha.

Active: Vidhi had not received the parcel.

Passive: The parcel had not been received by Vidhi.

Active: Vishal had solved the doubt.

Passive: The doubt had been solved.

Active: Had they caught the thief?

Passive: Had the thief been caught by them?

Active: I had paid fifty thousand.

Passive: Fifty thousand had been paid by me.

Active and Passive Voice Rules forFuture Simple Tense

You can check Active Voice and Passive Voice Rules chart for future simple tense.

Active Voice

Passive Voice

(Auxiliary Verb- will+ be)

Subject + will+ v1+ object.

Object+ will+ be +V3+ by + subject

Subject +will + not+ V1+object

Object + will+ not +be+V3+ by Subject

Will+ Subject + V1+ object+?

Will + Object+ be +v3+ by+ subject+?

We can better understand Rules of Active and Passive Voice with examples for future simple tense.

Active and Passive Voice Examples with Answers of Future Simple Tense

Active: Kriya will sew the bag.

Passive: The bag will be sewed by Kriya.

Active: Disha will not arrange the things.

Passive: The things will not be arranged by Disha.

Active: Will you mop the floor?

Passive: Will the floor be mopped by you?

Active: They will post the letter.

Passive: The letter will be posted.

Active: Reena will save money.

Passive: Money will be saved by Reena.

Active and Passive Voice Rules forFuture Perfect Tense

Here, we are sharing the Active Voice and Passive Voice Rules chart for future perfect tense.

Active Voice

Passive Voice

Subject + will+ have +v3+ object.

Object+ will+ have+ been +V3+ by + subject

Subject + will+ have +not+v3+ object.

Object + will+ have +not+been+v3+ subject

Will+ Subject+have+v3+ object+?

Will + object+have+been+v3+by +subject+?

Active and Passive Voice Exercises of Future Perfect Tense

Active: They will have brought the toy.

Passive: The toy will have been brought by them.

Active: Nimesh will not have changed the table cover.

Passive: The table cover will not have been changed by Nimesh.

Active: Will she have written the notes.

Passive: Will the notes have been written by her?

Active: They will have won the match.

Passive: The match will have been won by them.

Active: Vijay will have washed a shirt.

Passive: A shirt will have been washed by Vijay.

There is no Passive Voice formation for these tenses-

1.) Present Perfect Continuous Tense

2.) Past Perfect Continuous Tense

3.) Future Perfect Continuous Tense

4.) Future Continuous Tense

Exercise 1. Rewrite the following changing the active sentences to passive and passive sentences to active.

1. The thieves have been arrested by the police.

2. The marvelous performance delivered by the children enthralled us.

3. He has been invited to their party.

4. We have shipped your order.

5. The girl recited the poem beautifully.

6. The guests enjoyed the party.

7. The child impressed everyone with his polite manners.

8. A girl from Chennai won the first prize.

9. The readers like the latest book of the writer.

10. They are painting the walls.

11. The car has been fixed by the mechanic.

12. She accepted their invitation with pleasure.

Exercise 2. Change the active sentences below into passive sentences. Write "No change" if you think sentences cannot be changed.

1. She writes a letter.
2. They go to school every day.
3. He doesn`t paint the wall.
4. Why are you crying?
5. Did the mechanic fix your car?
6. You should do your homework.
7. Don`t talk so loudly.
8. They are painting their house.
9. We have drunk milk tea.
10. Will you watch TV tonight?
11. I am not going to work today.
12. He has been teaching English for ten years.
13. When are you going to buy a car?
14. Who taught you the active and passive sentences?
15. She had cleaned the kitchen.
16. We will have eaten dinner by the time you get there.
17. People speak English in the USA.
18. Would you rather learn English or French?
19. You must not come late to class.

20. She has to pass the test.
21. He bought his son a book.
22. Bismo teaches us every day.
23. Who is your teacher?
24. Who fights the coalition forces?
25. Who have you invited to the party?
26. I`ll build a hospital if I have a million dollars.
27. If I had had a million dollars, I would have built a big <u>mosque.</u>
28. We will be playing cricket at this time tomorrow.
29. Aren't they going to be building a house?
30. It has been raining since yesterday.
31. The explosion had killed many people.
32. I have never been to Egypt.
33. Have you been digging out the ground since morning?
34. I will have written a poem by the time you call me.
35. The heavy storm damaged a lot of crops in Mumbai.
36. I was playing football yesterday.
37. Could you help me, please?
38. Who can answer my question?
39. Will she have been watering the garden?
40. Milad is helping me solving the active and passive voice exercise.

CHAPTER FOURTEEN

Common Errors (Subject-verb Agreement)

Rule 1: A compound subject joined by 'and' generally takes a plural verb; as—

You and I are working.

Four and four make eight.

Are not your sister and brother ill?

Wealth and happiness are all Raj wants.

Bed and table were both very costly.

Rice and wheat, purchased a week ago, were both rotten.

Exceptions:

Rice and curry is his favourite dish.

Truth and honesty is the best policy.

Slow and steady wins the race.

Bread and butter is our daily need.

The crown and glory of life is character.

Rule 2:

Plural words that come in between a singular subject and its verb do not change the number of the subject as:

The sound of the bells was heard by everyone.

One of the books is missing.

The trouble with all those cars was slow speed.

Rule 3:

When words are added to a singular subject by with, together with, along with, in addition to, as well as, except, besides, and not, and no less than, the number of the subject remains singular as:

The ship with all its passengers was drowned.

The letter, together with other documents, was lost.

He, along with his parents, is coming today.

A watch in addition to ?50, was given to Hari.

Ram as well as Shyam was laughing.

No one except a few students was there.

Milk, besides vegetables is good for health.

Satish and not you, has passed.

He no less than his friends, is guilty.

Rule 4: When two subjects are joined by as well as, the verb agrees in number and person, with the first one; as

He, as well as they, is ready to jump.

My comrades, as well as I, are visiting Delhi.

Rule 5: When 2 or more nouns or pronouns in the singular or connected by, or or either or, neither nor, they take a singular verb:

Neither Raj nor his sister is to blame.

Either the dog or the cat has been killed.

Rule 6: When one of the subjects joined by or, nor either or neither nor is plural, The verb must be plural and plural subjects should be placed close to the verb as:

Either the former or his sons reap the harvest.

Neither Satish nor his sons are honest.

Rule 7: Windows subjects joined by or nor either or. Neither nor are of different persons, the verb agrees with the nearer subject as:

Either he or you are guilty.

Neither you nor I am to blame.

Neither you nor he is willing to come.

Neither he nor they are honest.

Rule 8: The indefinite pronouns many, a, each, each one, any, everyone, everybody, anybody, nobody, either, neither and no one take singular verbs as:

Many a flower is born in blush unseen.

Each of them was glad.

Everybody wants food.

Everyone who saw his dead body was moved.

Anybody with a will to work is welcome.

Nobody is willing to help me.

Either of the two books is sufficient.

No one likes to be criticised.

Every new born day is teeming with splendid chances.

Each one of you has to suffer for it.

Note: But in informal situations, especially, in conversation, and neither is often felt to be plural, especially when followed by some phrase like of them. The same usage applies to none:

Neither of my sisters are married.

None of my friends are interested in cricket.

Rule 9: When two nouns are qualified by each or every, although connected by and, they require a singular verb as:

Every boy and every girl was given sweets.

Each son and each daughter of Ram was educated.

Every day and every night brings its own pleasure.

Rule 10: Nouns qualified by each and every take singular verb as:

Every man and woman on this earth has to die one day.

Its soldier and sailor is to March.

It is assumed in the above sentences that the every before woman and the each before soldier are understood.

Rule 11: If the subject is a title, the name of a book, a clause, a quotation or other group of words expressing a single idea, the verb is singular; as:

Tales from Shakespeare' makes us an interesting reading.

Sparks is a well-known weekly.

'All men are created equal' is a truth.

The United States is a rich country.

'Hard Times' has been written by Dickens.

Rule 12: Sometimes the subject of a sentence, though plural in form, denotes some specific quality or amount or distance considered as a single unit. In all such cases the verb is generally singular; as:

Three thousand miles is a long distance.

Ten pounds is enough for me.

Ten years is sufficient to complete the project.

Three mounds of coal has been used.

Sixteen annas is equal to one rupee.

Five hours is not much for outdoor work.

Note: Sometimes a plural verb is used if the idea of plurality is dominant. When the subject says David Green, is a sum of money considered as a whole, the singular verb is used. When the subject is a sum of money and the reference is to the bills or coins considered separately, the plural verb is used; as:

There were ten gold coins in her briefcase.

A thousand rupees were distributed among the flood victims.

Five years have rolled by.

The first ten years were the most nerve-racking.

Rule 13. Some noun which are plural in form but singular in meaning, take a singular verb; as:

This news is not correct.

Economics is a difficult subject.

Ethics deals with the problem of morality.

Measles is a dangerous disease.

The wages of sin is death.

Note: Remember the following:

a. Physics, Mathematics, Politics, and Economics are singular when they refer to single branches of study.

b. Tactics and acrobatics are plural when they refer to physical activities.

a. The following words need special care:

1. Noun plural in form but singular in meaning

There are several nouns, plural in form but singular in meaning. They nearly always require singular verbs. Here is a list of such words:

    aeronautics aesthetics mumps

    Algiers ethics Naples

    alms gallows news

    analytics hydraulics optics

    Athens hydromechanics phonetics

    bellows innings physics

    billiards linguistics politics

    civics magnetics rickets

    dynamics metaphysics statistics

    economics measles summons

Look at some plural nouns that always take plural verbs. Here is the list:

    annals goods socks

    arms leavings spectacles

    ashes links thanks

    assets nuptials tidings

    auspices odds vitals

    clothes premises wages

    credentials proceeds wares

    customs remains scissors

    embers riches pliers

    environs riches trousers

    fetters savings glasses

Now look at these sets of words also:

Advice: counsel

Advices: commercial information

Air: atmosphere

Airs: assumed behaviour

Force: energy

Forces: armed men

Good: benefit

Goods: movable property

Iron: a metal

Irons: fetters made of iron

Return: coming back
Returns: statistics
Sand: a kind of matter
Sands: a tract of sandy land
Wood: timber
Woods: forest
Water: aqua/H_2O
Waters: waterbodies
Nouns having two meaning in the Plural against one in the singular:
Circumstance: fact
Circumstances: facts/condition
Colour: hue
Colours: hues/flag of a regiment
Custom: habit
Customs: habits/tax
Effect: result
Effects: results/goods and chattels
Manner: way
Manners: ways/behaviour
Pain: suffering
Pains: sufferings/trouble
Premise: a proposition in reasoning
Premises: proposition/buildings
Quarter: a fourth part
Quarters: fourth parts/lodgings
Nouns having two meanings in the Singular against one in the Plural:
Abuse: wrong use/reproach
Abuses: wrong uses
Foot: a part of the body/infantry
Feet: parts of the body
Gain: acquisition/profit
Gains: profits
Horse: an animal/cavalry

Horses: animals
Light: lamp/radiance
Lights: lamps
People: a nation/persons
Peoples: nations
Powder: mixtures/for guns
Powders: mixtures
Practice: habit/profession
Practices: habits
Nouns having two forms in the Plurals:
Cloths: material for making garments
Clothes: garment
Dies: stamps for coinage
Dice: small cubes used in games
Indexes: tables of contents
Indices: signs used in algebra
Shot: littles balls discharged from a gun
Shots: photographs
Staves: sticks/poles
Staffs: department in the army/business
Nouns having the same form for the Plural as for the Singular:
Deer:
Singular: This deer id beautiful.
Plural: these deer are fleet-footed.
Dozen;
Singular: He bought one dozen eggs.
Plural: He bought five dozen eggs.
Hundred:
Singular: Give me one hundred rupees.
Plural: There are four hundred students.
Sheep:
Singular: That is my sheep.
Plural: Those sheep are yours.
Stone:
Singular: He hit me with a stone.

Plural: He weighs ten stone.

Note: But when 'of' is used we say....... 'hundreds of boys', 'thousands of men', etc.

Rule 14: If the subject of a sentence begins with a fraction, the verb agrees with the noun or pronoun that comes after the preposition *of,* as:

Two-thirds of the book is interesting.

Two-thirds of the books are interesting.

A quarter of it is fresh.

A quarter of them are stale.

Rule 15: If the subject of a sentence begins with *A number of* , the verb will always be plural for *A number of* means *many* as:

A number of children are playing in the park.

A number of prisoners have escaped from jail.

But if the subject begins with *The number of*, the verb is always singular; as:

The number of children is very small.

The number of students in this college has swelled.

Rule 16: Phrases beginning with a number of, a chain of, a series of, a herd of, a batch of, a crowd of, a flock of, a bevy of, etc., take a singular verb though the word after *of* is plural; as:

A band of musician has given the best performance.

A bevy of beautiful ladies is going for ramp-walk.

A herd of cattle was grazing in the field.

A batch of student has been studying since the last four hours.

A crowd of people was playing the cards.

A flock of sheep has been killed by the wolves.

Rule 17: Some of the collective nouns take the verb in the singular or in the plural according as the speaker thinks of the thing as a single whole or of the individual of which it is composed as:

Class, Cabinet, Committee, Board, Army, Jury, Mob, Government, Team, etc., as:

The team is winning. (as a unit)

The team are trying hard to win. (as individuals)

The cabinet has taken decision for the welfare or the public. (as a unit)

The cabinet have decided to meet the next month. (as individuals)

The committee has given its report. (as a unit)

The committee are trying its best to justify the inquiry. (as individuals)

The jury is determined at its decision. (as a unit)

The jury are not equal in their decision. (as individuals)

The government is looking at the hike in fuel prices. (as a unit)

The government are introducing NEP from 2025. (as individuals)

Rule 18: Certain nouns though singular in form, are used as plural and they take plural verb; as:

The cattle are grazing in the field.

The landed gentry were once all in all.

The public were moved by this spectacle.

The clergy were unanimous in their opinion.

The vermin are harmful.

Note: 'People' is used both in singular and plural when it means a nation; as:

The Americans are a simple and brave people.

Many different peoples live in Asia.

Rule 19: The following nouns are used only in the singular form and the verb that follows them is also singular; as:

abuse, advice, alarm, alphabet, bread, brick, bunting, clothing, furniture, gossip, hair, information, issue, luggage, offspring, poetry, scenery, thunder, etc.

Wrong: The sceneries of Darjeeling are very beautiful.

Right: The scenery of Darjeeling is very beautiful.

Wrong: Their informations are based on facts.

Right: Their information is based on facts.

Wrong: All my furnitures have been burnt.

Right: All my furniture is burnt.

Wrong: Your hairs have turned grey.

Right: Your hair has turned grey.

Wrong: His luggages have been packed.

Right: His luggage has been packed.

Rule 20.: The subject of a sentence may begin with any one of the following phrases: a great deal of, a lot of, most of, and some of. In such a situation, the verb agrees with the object of the preposition 'of':

A good deal of time has been lost.

A good deal of efforts are needed.

Some of the music was boring.

Some of the children were hungry.

Rule 21: When 'and' connects two or more titles or designations of the same person, the verb is always singular; as:

The Principal and Secretary is on leave.

The Governor of Bihar and Chancellor of this university has given this directive.

Rule 22: If the subject of a sentence begins with None of, the verb is generally plural; as:

None of the candidates have appeared for an interview.

None of these scientists are willing to take up this challenge.

Rule 23: If none refers to an uncountable noun, the verb is singular. If it refers to countable noun in its plural form the verb can be either singular or plural; as:

I have been waiting for the sugar but none of it has arrived.

I have been waiting for my friends but none of them have arrived.

Rule 24: Certain adjectives are used with the definite article to talk about group of people in a particular condition; as:

The blind, the rich, the poor, the sick, the young, the old, the dead, the brave, the coward, the handicapped, the unemployed, etc.

These expressions have a plural meaning; 'the blind' means 'the blind people' or 'all blind people'.

The blind are helpless.

The rich are selfish.

The poor are hungry.

The unemployed are restless.

Rule 25: Some of thenationality words ending in -sh or -ch or -ese can also be used with a definite article; as:

The British, The English, The French, The Irish, The Dutch

These expressions are plural 'the British' means all 'the British people'.

The French love good food.

The Japanese are hard-working.

The British have a long history.

The Chinese are strong willed.

Rule 26: (a) When the a or an is used after Many, the noun that follows it is always singular and consequently the verb is also singular; as:

Many a man comes and goes.

Many an animal lives on grass.

(b) The collocation More than one is treated as a compound of one. As a singular noun, it is followed by a singular verb; as:

More than one passenger was killed.

Many than one examinee was expelled.

Here you cannot use passengers or examinees in place of passenger or examinee, nor you can use were in place of was.

(c)In the sentence pattern More + plural noun + than one... the verb is always plural; as:

More principals than one were present.

More books than one have been burnt.

Rule 27: In ex pressions where the same singular noun is joined by a preposition, the verb used is always singular; as:

Ship after ship is heading towards the shore.

Letter after letter pinpoints the need for hard work.

Rule 28: When clauses are introduced by the relative, pronouns who, whom, whose, which, or that, the verb agrees with the antecedent of the relative pronoun in person and number; as:

He made a list of things that were required.

I like a boy who shows intelligence.

I like people who are honest.

The book which is on the table is not mine.

Rule 29: There can never be the subject of a verb. Hence look for the subject after the verb in sentences beginning with there; as:

There are always two sides of every story.

There were ten students in our group.

There seem to be three lions in the den.

There is a book on the table.

Rule 30: When a sentence is built around a linking verb, the verb must agree with the subject; as:

The most difficult thing is the adjectives.

Exercises

i.   Choose the correct ones:

1.   The man and woman (is/are) determined to tell the truth.
2.   The horse and carriage (is/are) ready.
3.   Five and five (make/makes) ten.
4.   Churchill, statesman and writer, (is/are) no more.
5.   The house with its contents (was/were) burnt down.
6.   The father as well as the son (is/are) absent.
7.   Dick, together with his friends (was/were) drowned.
8.   Neither Ram nor Gauri (is/are) criminal.
9.   Every railway coolie (carry/carries) license.
10. Neither he nor I (are/am) wrong.
11. My friends as well as I (was/were) given books.
12. Each of the wounded soldiers (was/were) given first aid.
13. Either the waiter of the cook (was/were) dishonest.
14. Neither of the plans (was/were) approved.
15. The jury (was/were) divided in the matter.
16. A jury (consist/consists) of twelve persons.
17. Everyone of these hostelers (is/are) absent.
18. Physics (is/are) difficult subject.
19. *Tales from Tagore* is nice collection of stories.
20. Twenty miles(is/are) a long distance.
21. My means (is/are) limited.

22. Great pains (has/have) been taken to obtain permit.
23. By (these/this) means, I hope to succeed.
24. The introduction of reforms (was/were) not liked by him.
25. The state of affairs (is/are) sure to affect his career.
26. I ate four (bread/loaves).
27. He gave me good (advices/advice).
28. His house is built of (brick/bricks).
29. He has written a (poem/poetry)
30. My college has Italian (furniture/furnitures).

ii. Supply a verb in agreement with its subject:

1. The horse and cart .... at his door.
2. Three Musketeers .... written by Alexander Dumas.
3. One of the books ...... missing.
4. Bread and milk .... wholesome food.
5. The officer along with his clerks .... in the office.
6. The Prime Minister as well as his entire cabinet .... there.
7. The President and member ex-officio ..... in the meeting.
8. The philosopher and the statesman .... required.
9. My friend as well as I ,,,,, joining the army.
10. Neither Ram nor his relatives ...... coming to my place.
11. Either of the two boys ...... willing to work.
12. Nobody .... helping me.
13. Ten dollars ...... enough for me.
14. Mumps ..... a dangerous disease.
15. I like a man who .... laborious.
16. I made a list of things that .... needed.
17. There ...... two hundred students in my class.
18. The cattle .... grazing in the field.
19. ..... there anybody in the office? No, there .... no one.
20. The data .... Incorrect.

15
Words Followed by Appropriate Prepositions

1. My younger sister has been admitted to class I.
2. The manager did not agree to my proposal.
3. Everybody will agree with me that we should not waste time.
4. All of us agree on this point.
5. Two hours a week have been allotted to yoga.
6. I am amazed at the courage shown by this little child.
7. He was angry with me for not writing to him earlier.
8. He was angry at being kept waiting.
9. She was annoyed with her son for behaving so stupidly.
10. She was annoyed at her son's stupid behaviour.
11. The child is quite safe. You need not feel anxious for/about him.
12. Priya apologised to her teacher for not submitting the assignment on time.
13. The accused appealed to the judge for a lenient view.
14. She has applied to the principal for leave.
15. Don't argue with me on this issue; my decision is final.
16. The train has already arrived at the station.
17. Let me assure you of my full support.
18. His father was astonished at his brilliant result.
19. Please attend to what I say.
20. We have a nurse to attend upon my aged mother.
21. You should avail yourself of every opportunity.
22. She begged money off me.
23. He begged for help but did not get any.
24. Many people do not believe in taking medicines.
25. I don't believe you.
26. Why are you bent on disturbing me?
27. In his old age, he was blessed with his son.
28. Being blind of one eye, he could not get a driving licence.
29. Mothers are sometimes blind to the faults of their children.
30. He boasts of being the best cricketer in the team.
31. The authorities charged him with neglecting his duty.
32. The principal's residence is close to the school building.
33. 2 cars collided with each other and overturned.

34. I complained to the teacher of the head boy's rudeness with me.
35. I have already complained against the peon.
36. The child has been cured of malaria.
37. I did not know how to deal with an armed dacoit.
38. We do not deal in stationery at this shop.
39. You can depend on my help.
40. A saint has no desire for worldly goods.
41. Very few people die of malaria now.
42. The old man died from a fall.
43. The soldier died from a vote.
44. How many people can die for their country?
45. We have disposed of our land.
46. The King disposed of all his enemies.
47. The property was equally divided between the two men.
48. Divide these sweets among yourselves.
49. Divide this line into two parts.
50. When I was abroad, I often dreamt of my own country.
51. His failure was due to his own carelessness.
52. The cost of this pen is equal to that of five good pencils.
53. We should always remain faithful to our country.
54. Famous for the Taj Mahal.
55. I can fight with anyone for a friend.
56. We must not fight against our own people.
57. The policemen fired at the dacoit.
58. Children are usually fond of chocolates.
59. I know your fondness for chocolates.
60. West Indians are very good at cricket.
61. It's very good of you to help me at this critical time.
62. He was good to me as long as I stayed with him.
63. I'm grateful to you for your kind help.
64. He was held guilty of misleading the police.
65. Many people become hard of hearing in their old age.
66. Have faith in God and hope for the best.
67. I'm hopeful of a good result.

68. Indian goods are no longer inferior to imported goods.
69. Nobody informed me of your being unwell.
70. The teacher inquired of me the cause of my absence.
71. The police is inquiring into the matter.
72. She insisted on consulting a doctor immediately.
73. Is there someone interested in buying my stamp collection?
74. If you interfere with him, he'll be offended.
75. One should never interfere in others affairs.
76. I invited all my friends to my birthday party.
77. Don't feel jealous of others' wealth.
78. We found the offer so good that we immediately jumped at it.
79. Though Mrs Khanna is junior to others, she is our best teacher.
80. Hardworking is the key to success.
81. In the dark, she knocked against a chair.
82. Someone is knocking at the door.
83. This road leads to the police station.
84. He longed for the company of a good friend.
85. We ought to be loyal to our country.
86. In wrestling, you are no match for him.
87. At school, Gandhiji was always obedient to his teachers.
88. They objected to my presence in the room.
89. She was overcome with grief at his failure.
90. My parents were pleased with me for winning the first prize.
91. Sachin is very popular with his teammates.
92. I prefer classical dance to folk dance.
93. The chief minister presided over our annual function.
94. His parents prevented him from joining the army.
95. Hema takes pride in her good looks.
96. Hema is proud of her good look.
97. He quarrelled with his brother over property.
98. Miss Mathur is very quick at typing.
99. Students should always be respectful to their teachers.
100. My case has been referred to the principal.
101. Our country is rich in minerals.

102.   The dacoits robbed him of all his money.
103.   Ashok ruled over his people with love and kindness.
104.   The teacher was fully satisfied with my answers.
105.   I am searching for my last books.
106.   Alok has high fever, kindly send for the doctor.
107.   Our examination is approaching and we are running short of time.
108.   I am sick at heart.
109.   I'm now sick of his long waiting.
110.   These two figures are similar to each other.
111.   Though he was himself responsible for his troubles, yet we felt sorry for him.
112.   At last, he succeeded in buying a good pre-owned car.
113.   Your watch appears to be superior to buy.
114.   Are you sure of the help of your friends?
115.   Everybody sympathised with me in my misfortunes.
116.   I have no taste for sports like boxing.
117.   Are not you tired of leading such an ideal life?
118.   The old man got tired with working so long.
119.   If you make a promise, be true to it.
120.   Don't put your trust in total strangers.
121.   All his colleagues decided to vote for or against him.
122.   I have been waiting for you for a very long time.
123.   A nurse is always waiting on her.
124.   I often wonder at Gandhiji's achievements through violence.
125.   His behaviour is worthy of high praise.

Exercise 1. Fill in the blanks with appropriate prepositions:

1.   He aimed .... becoming a dentist.
2.   The police wrongly charged him .... Murder.
3.   You need not feel anxious ..... my welfare.
4.   If you had availed yourself ...... that offer, you would have risen high in life.
5.   Students complained ..... the poor food provided in the hostel.

6. She always dreamt ...... becoming an accomplish dancer.
7. The judge held him guilty .... theft.
8. The doctor insisted ..... performing the operation immediately.
9. I take pride ..... being an Indian.
10. Your complaint was referred .... the higher authorities.

Exercise 2: Fill in the blanks with appropriate preposition:

1. Your essay is worthy ...... the first prize.
2. Our bus collided ..... a van.
3. The blind man knocked .... a wall.
4. I requested my neighbour to send ...... a doctor.
5. He appealed ...... the High Court......... the decision of the DM.
6. He might have been blind ..... an eye but he was not blind ..... his weaknesses.
7. If you are dealing .... jewellery, you may have to deal ...... different customers.

Exercise 3: Fill in the blanks with one of the prepositions given in the brackets:

1. The whole class agreed ..... this point. (at, on, with)
2. Do you have any trust .... God? (in, on, over)
3. We warned the driver ...... the danger ahead. (for, against, of)
4. I enquired .... him about your address. (from, of, with)
5. Imported goods are no longer superior....... goods made in India. (to, from, than)
6. They were quarrelling ...... an ordinary matter. (on, at, over)
7. Neha is always boasting ...... her intelligence. (about, on, of)
8. King Humayun died....... a fall. (of, with, from)
9. One should always take care ..... one's health. (for, of, about)
10. My father was very angry ...... me. (at, to, with)

Exercise 4: Fill in the blanks with appropriate prepositions:

Gautam was born........poor parents. His life was full.......hardships but he never complained ....anything. Some children of his class were quite rich but he was not jealous .... them. He worked hard and succeeded ....winning a scholarship. During the college days also, he was always.........the top. His parents felt proud ....him. But he always remained simple. He never boasted ...... his achievements.